Mary Gorman

Lovebirds

Everything About Purc... ...
and Health

Filled with Full-c... ...graphs
Illustrations by Michele Earle-Bridges

BARRON'S

CONTENTS

BEFORE YOU BUY

*There are few things cuter than a lovebird.
A healthy, active lovebird is a tail-waggling,
feathered ball of energy with a twinkle in its
eye. One of the smallest members of the parrot
family, lovebirds can make colorful, lively,
interactive pets. But several myths about
lovebirds persist—that they are delicate, that a
lovebird kept without a partner will soon die of
a broken heart, that they are "low-maintenance"
pets or merely useful as a decorator accessory.*

What Is a Lovebird?

Lovebirds are small parrots that are native to central and southcentral Africa and the island of Madagascar. They range in size from 5½ to 7 inches (14–17 cm) and come in a wide variety of colors. There are nine different species of lovebird, three of which are generally readily available as pets. Although in some species the males and females are visibly different from each other, most species of lovebirds that are available as pets are sexually monomorphic, which means you can't tell a male from a female just by looking.

Despite their small size, lovebirds are very active and have high-octane personalities. Everything they do—eating, bathing, playing, or interacting—they do with gusto. They can be very stubborn at times, and do not hesitate

*There are few things cuter than a happy,
healthy lovebird.*

to make their desires known. They have a tendency to be nippy when they want something, and those small beaks can pack a pretty mean pinch!

Lovebirds are *not* low maintenance. Their cages need to be cleaned often (biweekly is good; daily is even better), and their diets should include a daily selection of fresh fruits and vegetables, chopped or shredded to accommodate their small beaks. They need daily interaction with their owners for their own well-being and should be handled every day whenever possible. Since they tend to hide signs of illness until they are at death's door, they should be watched carefully and weighed weekly to monitor for sudden weight loss, one of the earliest symptoms of illness. Annual veterinary visits with a certified avian veterinarian are also recommended. Healthy, well-protected lovebirds may have a life span of up to 15 to 20 years or more.

Although lovebirds are small, they are neither meek nor gentle. Lovebirds are active, stubborn, and not afraid to let their desires be known. They are energetic and need careful supervision when out of their cages, because they have no concept of what possessions are valuable to you, and will follow their instincts when it comes to chewing, shredding, and rearranging your belongings, particularly those that are made of wood and paper.

Although they are not without their challenges, happy, healthy, well-adjusted lovebirds are a delight to their owners. They see every day as an adventure and greet it with a twinkle in their eye and a swagger in their step. When they play, they play hard, attacking their toys and ringing their bells with gusto. Tame lovebirds enjoy spending time with their owner, preening the owner's hair and getting the owner to preen their head feathers in return, sharing snacks and exploring the nooks and crannies of their owner's clothing.

Pet lovebirds require a fairly good-sized commitment of time and energy, but in return, make entertaining and engaging companions.

Should You Get a Lovebird?

There are many reasons why one might want to get a pet lovebird—and just as many reasons not to. Owning a lovebird requires a long-term commitment—a healthy, well-cared-for lovebird can live for up to 20 years or more!

The Truth About Birds

Owning a bird is quite different than owning a dog or a cat. Dogs and cats are familiar to most people, so it is easy to interpret what a wagging tail or fur standing on end means. Birds are not as easily understood. While they do have their own body language, it is not as easy to interpret (see the special section, Understanding Your Lovebird, for more on this topic). Both parrots and the people who interact with them can become frustrated when things don't happen the way they anticipated. Parrots may become frustrated and will bite as a way of expressing it. People may become frustrated and begin to neglect their birds.

It is possible to have a rewarding owner-pet relationship with your lovebird, but it is something at which one has to work. It's not enough simply to provide food and shelter; you have to engage, interact, and to some extent, entertain your bird on a daily basis. In short, owning even a small bird requires a really big commitment.

Lovebirds and Children

Some birds make great pets for a gentle, responsible child. Lovebirds are not one of them. Despite their small size and cute appearance, lovebirds can be very aggressive and may

Pairs or Singles?

Although lovebirds are one of the smallest parrots, they are fairly hardy birds that, for the most part, breed easily in captivity and that are readily available as pets. There is a myth that lovebirds have to be kept in pairs lest the singly kept lovebird die of a broken heart, but this isn't true—in fact, single lovebirds generally make better pets than paired lovebirds because all of their attention and interest becomes focused on their owner rather than on the other bird.

Factors to Consider

Pros	Cons
✔ A compact size	✔ Active birds that require a fairly large living space
✔ Available in a wide variety of bright colors	
✔ Big personality in a small package	✔ Require a varied diet including fruits and vegetables for optimum health (not just seed)
✔ Relatively quiet compared to other parrots	
✔ Relatively low priced	✔ May be difficult to tame or nippy
✔ A hand-tamed lovebird can be an affectionate, interactive pet	✔ Lovebirds can be aggressive chewers and may damage woodwork or shred papers if given the opportunity

deliver a fairly hard bite. For these reasons, I would not recommend a lovebird as a pet intended for a child under the age of 12. Other species of birds, such as cockatiels, make much more suitable, affectionate, and interactive pets for children who are old enough to handle them responsibly.

Lovebirds and Other Pets

Lovebirds tend to be aggressive birds that do not seem to realize that they are actually quite diminutive, and they may exhibit no fear around other pets. This can be a setup for a potential disaster, particularly if your other pet happens to be a dog, cat, or ferret. Lovebirds should never be allowed out of their cage if one of these other animals is around. To do so is to court disaster, particularly in the case of cats; they not only prey on birds instinctively, but their saliva contains a type of bacteria that is toxic to parrots, so that even if you do manage to rescue the bird from the cat, if it has been bitten, it may die from the resulting

bacterial infection unless prompt medical intervention is given.

Lovebirds and Other Birds

Lovebirds tend to be aggressive with all but their own lovebird species, and should never share cage space with a non-lovebird. They will attack and possibly even kill what they see as an intruder to their space. Size is not a deterrent—lovebirds will attack a bird as large as a macaw, apparently with no idea that doing so puts their own lives at risk. Mixing a lovebird with another lovebird can also be a dicey proposition. If the second lovebird is a different species than the first, they may or may not be able to get along.

As a general rule, two males or a male and a female have the best chances of getting along eventually, but two females tend to be more cantankerous and may fight to the point where they need to be separated, although this can vary from bird to bird. If introducing a male to a female, it's best to go with an older male, as the females are more likely to attack a young male.

EQUIPMENT

It's a good idea to buy all of the equipment you are going to need and have everything set up before you purchase your bird in order to make its transition into your home as smooth as possible. Make choices that both you and your bird will be happy with, particularly when it comes to the bird's cage and its furnishings.

Cage Requirements

Because they are very active, lovebirds need a cage that allows them plenty of room to move around. Cages that are 20 inches by 20 inches (51 cm by 51 cm) or larger work well. Just as important as the dimensions of the cage perimeter is the amount of space that exists between the bars—they should be no more than ½ inch (1.2 cm) apart, and may be arranged either vertically or horizontally or in a combination of both. Cages with corners tend to make the bird feel more secure and provide more floor space than round cages. Resist the urge to make do with an old cage that you find at a yard sale, or that you have left over from your mother's parakeet—many older cages may contain exposed zinc or lead, metals that can be toxic if they get into the bird's digestive system. Cages marketed as appropriate for cock-

A heavy blue pied peach-faced lovebird.

atiels are generally suitable in terms of size and bar spacing for a single lovebird.

Because some lovebirds get very territorial about "defending" their cages, make sure that you get a cage with separate doors over each of the food dishes, so that you won't have to reach inside the cage to service the dishes when the bird is feeling the need to defend its "turf." Cages today are available in a wide variety of shapes, sizes, and colors, and you may wish to buy one that matches either your décor or your bird, but study the cage critically before you buy it. Sides that bow out beyond the perimeter of the base may look attractive, but also allow food, feathers, and droppings to fall on your floor or furniture rather than onto the tray at the bottom of the cage.

Note: Because birds fly horizontally rather than vertically, a cage that is longer and wider than it is tall is best because it allows the birds more room to fly and exercise.

Perches

There should be a variety of perches, set at different heights within the cage. The perches should come in different diameters so that the foot has to flex into various positions in order for the bird to perch. This is a much healthier arrangement than having several versions of the same perch, which would mean that the bird's foot must always be in the same position any time it is perched, resulting in an atrophy of the foot muscles. Perches come in a wide variety of different materials: wood, plastic, natural branches, even concrete. Perches made of concrete or covered with sandpaper are marketed as being good for the bird's feet because they will help to keep the toenails filed down. These are helpful to an extent, but may also irritate the feet if they are the only types of perches that you provide for the bird to stand on; they should be used as a supplemental perch rather than an exclusive one.

Perches should be placed in the cage in such a way that the bird does not sit directly over the food and water dishes because, in such an arrangement, the bird will probably defecate

Dishes should be placed away from perches to avoid having the food become soiled.

into the food and water supply, creating an unhealthy situation.

Dishes

The food and water dishes should be kept clean at all times. The material that the dishes are made from is not important as long as they do not contain zinc or lead or some other potentially toxic substance. Plastic, stainless steel, and ceramic (without a lead-based glaze) are all fine. The lower the dishes are placed within the cage, the less likely the husks of the seed are to fall outside the cage. Some cages come with seed-catcher skirts around the base of the cage to keep the mess contained, and there are commercially produced elastic-edged cloths you can place around the cage to keep the mess contained, although the latter may obscure your view of the bird.

If you opt for a dish that rests inside a metal ring attached to the side of the cage, be sure to remove the ring attachment when you take the dish out for cleaning, or take the bird with you when you are washing the dish. There are reports of lovebirds becoming stuck or injured while exploring the empty ring. Lovebirds are curious, active pets—if there's a potential for trouble, they'll probably find it.

Number of Dishes

It's best to have three separate dishes for your lovebirds—even more if you keep more than one bird to a cage. One dish should be used for water. Use your own discretion as to the quality of the tap water in your neighborhood; if you drink it, then it should be fine for the birds, but if for some reason you find it unpalatable, then bottled water may be the

A lightly pied lovebird.

best option. One dish should be used for a commercially prepared food mix, and the last dish should be used for fresh fruits and vegetables and the occasional treat. This last dish should be used only part of the day because chopped fruits and vegetables left out at room temperature spoil quickly and become breeding grounds for potentially harmful bacteria. Such foods should be left in the cage for no more than an hour or two, then removed, and the dish should be thoroughly cleaned.

Toys

A lovebird needs a good selection of toys to keep it happy and busy, and to help keep its beak in shape. The toys should not be so numerous or arranged in such a way that they impede the bird's ability to fly from one end of the cage to the other. The toys should be durable, not made of light plastic, as are many of the toys intended for budgies (parakeets). A lovebird's beak is much stronger than that of a budgie and they may be able to break apart the plastic, possibly ingesting some of the small pieces and causing severe internal injuries.

The best toys are colorful (birds, like people, can perceive color), durable, interesting, and made of bird-safe materials. Toys designed for cockatiel-sized birds are best. Owners have the option of either buying a ready-made toy or making their own toys out of individual parts. Toys with wooden parts are good because they

The old story that lovebirds must be kept in pairs is untrue. In fact, single lovebirds often make the best pets.

provide an opportunity for the bird to chew and keep its beak worn down. Toys that the birds can swing on are also a big favorite. Bells also seem to be very popular with the birds, but only bells with a clapper should be used; the round, "jingle bell" type of bell with the slits in it is not a safe option, because the bird's beak, tongue, or toes may get caught in the slit, resulting in severe blood loss or other injury. If a bell is used as part of a toy, the owner should frequently check the clapper, tugging on it to make sure that it is firmly attached so that there's no risk that it will break off and become accidentally ingested.

Keeping several different toys and rotating them so that they are not all offered at the same time helps to keep things interesting for the bird. Having six toys and keeping three of them in the cage, and swapping one of them every week helps to keep the bird from becoming bored.

Foot Toys

Toys that don't hang or mount on the side of the cage—called "foot toys"—are not the best option for lovebirds, whose legs are set too far back on their bodies to be used as "hands" the way some bigger parrots do. Leaving foot toys on the bottom of the cage may result in the

The ideal location for the cage is one where the lovebird can see and be seen.

Toys are essential to keep your lovebird from becoming bored.

Two Fischer's lovebirds.

A lovebird should be an interactive member of the family.

toys being defecated on, which is very unsanitary. Foot toys can be tied from the cage walls or ceiling so that the bird can play with them, even though it is unable to hold them.

Wooden Toys

Wooden toys are the best option because they can be chewed on, but this means that the toys will become worn and have to be replaced on occasion. Toys made of Lucite, hard plastic, or metal are other good options. If a toy becomes worn, it can be taken apart and the good pieces can be used to construct a new toy using rawhide strips, shoelaces, or cotton rope to hold them together. Making bird toys is also a great way of involving children in caring for your lovebird. My own daughter loves to make toys for our lovebird out of old toy parts, popsicle sticks, beads, old keys, and other bird-safe objects.

Many pet stores carry unstrung, colored, wooden blocks and beads intended specifically for making bird toys. Wood can also be colored at home using food coloring or a packet of instant unsweetened juice mix or powdered Jell-O mix combined with a tablespoon of water. Let the wood soak in the juice mix, dry, and then they're ready for the birds.

Location

Where you put the cage can be just as important as the cage itself. Lovebirds are very social animals that do not like to be alone. The best place for the cage is a highly trafficked part of the house where the bird can see its human family and where it's easy for family members to stop and interact with it. If the bird is going to be placed in the same room with another pet bird, it's important to leave a good deal of space between cages. Lovebirds can be very aggressive when it comes to defending their "territory" and will bite the

Lovebirds need a roomy cage that is stocked to meet their needs.

on you, the theory goes, then it will become more aggressive with you. Even if you don't buy into this theory of bird's social hierarchies, you will make more frequent eye contact with your bird and thus enhance your relationship if you don't have to look up to see it.

Light

Just as humans can absorb vitamin D through sunlight, parrots can absorb vitamin D_3 through exposure to ultraviolet light. Vitamin D_3 is especially important in helping these birds absorb calcium, which in turn results in stronger bones and better overall health. Having your bird exposed to sunlight that comes into the room through a window does not expose the bird to the necessary ultraviolet light because the glass in the window filters the ultraviolet light so that it does not reach your bird.

In a warm climate, this can be remedied by opening the window so that the light comes in through the screen rather than the glass and then placing the bird so that the cage is half in/half out of the direct sunlight, which will allow the bird to move to the shady portion of the cage if it becomes overheated. If you live in a cooler climate, you can buy a specially designed, full-spectrum electric light that will emit the ultraviolet light that your lovebird needs to maintain optimum health during the winter months. This is a different kind of light from the ordinary, incandescent, fluorescent, or neon lights that don't emit ultraviolet light. Full-spectrum lights are available in pet stores

toes of any bird that dares to land upon their cage while they're inside it.

While being in a draft will not necessarily result in the death of a lovebird, the bird will not like sitting in a draft any more than you would, so the cage should be placed in a warm, draft-free part of the room. Lovebirds enjoy being near a window as long as they are not in direct sunlight at the hottest part of the day.

The cage should be set in a place where it is not likely to be bumped, but it should not be hung from the ceiling or placed so that the top of the cage is higher than the owner's eye level. There are some who feel that in the wild, the most important members of the flock occupy the highest places in the trees, so they will try to dominate and intimidate those they look down on. If your bird constantly looks down and pet supply catalogs and will say "full-spectrum" on the package.

The light should be set up so that both the light and its cord are well out of the bird's reach. The package directions will tell you exactly how to set up the light to best meet your bird's needs.

Cuttlebones and Mineral Blocks

Cuttlebones and mineral blocks are not only both good sources of calcium, but will also help to keep a lovebird's beak worn down to a comfortable level. Although both sexes can benefit from them, these are particularly important for females; they need the extra calcium because they may occasionally lay eggs, even if there is no male bird present (see page 77).

Gravel and Grit

In the old days, pet stores used to advise that you needed to provide a pet bird with a supply of gravel or grit to help the bird's crop break down the food. While this is true of some birds, such as chickens and turkeys, this isn't the case with lovebirds.

Grit is only necessary for birds that swallow their seeds whole; it helps to break down the outer husks of the shells and allows the birds to digest the inside of the seed. But parrots, including lovebirds, will remove the shell of their seed with their beaks before they swallow it, dropping the empty husk back into the food dish or onto the cage floor, so lovebirds do not require gravel or grit. In fact, giving these to a lovebird can be dangerous—there have been cases in which the grit had become clogged inside the bird's digestive tract, resulting in a fatal obstruction.

Lovebirds at a Glance

Generic Name	Genus: *Agapornis* (Selby 1836); Family: *Psittacidae*
Distribution	Africa, Madagascar, and some offshore islands
Number of Species	Nine:
	The Sexually Dimorphic Group:
	(1) *taranta*
	(2) *cana*
	(3) *pullaria*
	The Intermediate Group:
	(4) *roseicolis*
	(5) *swinderniana*
	The White Eye-ring Group
	(6) *lilianae*
	(7) *nigrigenis*
	(8) *fischeri*
	(9) *personata*
Size	5.1–6.7 inches (13–17 cm)
Longevity	10–12 years, possibly longer
Number of Eggs (Clutch)	3–8; usually 4–5, rarely more
Incubation Period	23–25 days; hens usually start brooding after the second egg has been laid; males may join hens in nest
Young (chicks) Leave Nest	38–50 days
Young Independent	About 14 days after leaving the nest

YOUR LOVEBIRD'S DIET

One thing you can do to help make your new lovebird's transition into your home easier is to continue to feed the bird the same food it was given at its previous place. You can switch to another brand later if you wish, but having a familiar food can be a source of comfort to a bird that is in the midst of experiencing a major upheaval.

Pellets

Pet birds traditionally ate a diet of bird seed. At the time, it was the best option available. The problem is that seeds tend to be high in fat and offer only a limited amount of vitamins and minerals. Recent years, however, have seen the development of pellets, a manufactured food that is less fattening and more complete in nutrition than an all-seed diet.

Although some people are reluctant to feed their lovebirds an all-pellet diet because some pellets have been associated with the development of visceral gout in some other types of parrots, pellets offer the most complete source of nutrition available. And many veterinarians recommend a pelleted diet. It is generally more expensive than seed, but there is less waste because, unlike seeds, where the shells and husks are discarded, the entire pellet can be eaten.

Some lovebirds seem to be reluctant to eat a pelleted diet. Instructions for converting the

A healthy diet means a longer, happier life.

bird from a seed diet to a pelleted one are included on most packages of pellets, but the owner needs to be vigilant in making sure that the bird takes to his new food.

Seed Mixes

It was once believed that all a pet bird needed to eat was birdseed, usually a millet-based mix with sunflowers and a few other types of grain. While this was usually sufficient to keep the bird alive for a few years, your bird will live longer, be healthier, and generally will be happier if you feed it a more balanced, varied diet consisting of pellets, seed, and fresh vegetables and/or fruit.

There are several different commercial brands of seed mix available from which the lovebird owner can choose. The name on the package is not nearly as important as its contents, and a brand that offers a wide variety of different seeds and grains is preferable to one that is mostly millet.

"Heat and Eat" Mixes

One convenient way to prepare "heat and eat" mixes is to cook the whole package at once and then put most of the mix into ice cube trays. Once they are frozen, pop the food cubes out and store them in a plastic freezer bag, then heat one a day in the microwave to feed to your bird. The ice cube-sized portions are just right for a lovebird's daily serving.

The best seed mixes are ones that either specify that they are intended for lovebirds, or say "small hookbill" on the outside of the package. Mixes intended for large hookbills consist of many ingredients that are either too big or too hard to be eaten easily by a lovebird-sized beak.

Look for an expiration date on the package—foods whose expiration dates have passed are more likely to have spoiled, be bug infested, or to have lost much of the nutritional value of the seeds. Seed and seed mixes intended for wild birds should not be given to pet birds because they are more likely to be past the expiration date, are less likely to be clean, and are intended for birds with different nutritional needs than your tropical African lovebird.

"Heat and Eat" Mixes

"Heat and eat" foods are mixes of dried grains, pastas, fruits, and vegetables that are cooked in water until they are soft, then given warm to the birds to eat. These are enormously popular with most lovebirds and can be supplemented with the addition of fresh or frozen fruits and vegetables that are added to the mix either before or after cooking for additional variety and nutrition. These mixes also have the advantage of portion control—the owner can either prepare a small amount at a time, or can cook the entire package and freeze the excess.

Water

Wild lovebirds are almost always found close to a source of water, which they not only drink but bathe in regularly. It's essential that your bird has continual access to a clean, fresh supply of water at all times. One thing to watch out for, however, is birds that like to make "soup" by dropping things into their food dishes. Although the bird may seem to think that this is a fine thing to do, it increases the chances of bacterial contamination in the water. So if your bird turns out to be a "soup maker" you will need to check its water supply several times a day, removing and cleaning out the water dish every time you find it full of things other than water. If your bird does not do this, changing the water daily should suffice.

Fruits and Vegetables

Whether you choose to feed your bird a commercial seed mix or a pelleted diet, supplementing these with a daily assortment of fruits and vegetables will make for a happier, healthier pet. Vegetables tend to be more readily eaten by lovebirds than fruit and are slightly better for them from a nutritional standpoint. It is especially important to provide vegetables

Lovebirds come in a variety of colors.

that are rich in vitamin A, such as yellow and dark green leafy varieties.

Fruits and vegetables intended for your bird can be purchased in a variety of forms—fresh, frozen, dried, or even canned. You can either share your daily portion with the bird (being careful not to give it anything that has been in contact with your mouth or contains salt, both of which would be potential health risks for the bird), give it the leftover vegetables from your dinner, or buy its favorites in the produce section of your local grocery store.

Caution: As with your own food, make sure to wash what you feed to your bird before it is eaten.

TIP

Salad Bars

Salad bars are a particularly good place to get a wide variety of foods for just pennies because you can buy the food in very small, lovebird-sized portions; a bit of shredded carrot, a few sprouts, a leaf of spinach, a ring of pepper, a pea pod, and a cube of melon weigh next to nothing and would provide a good variety of tastes and nutrients for your bird.

Fresh food should not be left in the cage for more than an hour or two. Food left in the bird's dish is at room temperature and may wilt and spoil, as potentially harmful bacteria breed on the warm, moist surfaces. After the bird has had sufficient time to eat, the fresh food dish should be removed, the contents discarded, and the dish should be thoroughly washed.

Meat

There is some controversy as to whether or not meat is a beneficial addition to a lovebird's diet. Some argue that wild lovebirds eat the occasional insect because they need the resulting protein. Other people feel that wild lovebirds are primarily vegetarian and do not need meat. Both groups agree that if meat is given, it should make up a very small portion of the total diet, offered maybe once or twice a week. They can be given a small amount of chicken or, if you want to go more "natural," you can buy a mealworm at your local pet store and offer it to your bird.

Some breeders swear by feeding their lovebirds mealworms, but my own experience was not so positive—I put a live mealworm in Doodle's cage and nothing I could do encouraged her to even look at the bug in her dish. The mealworm, meanwhile, crawled merrily over the seed and out of the dish. Afraid it would be just a matter of time before it made it out of the cage as well, I removed the creepy crawly critter from the cage and out of the house. It was just as well. I felt quite guilty at the idea of buying live food, and after that one experience, I've never had the urge to buy more.

Vitamin Supplements

When you go to the pet store, you may notice that there are several different types of vitamin supplements available for birds, and you may wonder if it would be a good idea to buy some

(opposite page)

top left: A peach-faced lovebird ready to eat.

top right: A white masked lovebird.

bottom: Normal Fischer's (left) and yellow Fischer's lovebirds.

An ideal diet includes daily servings of fruits and vegetables.

Average Composition of Some Commonly Used Vegetables for Lovebirds

Per 100 g consumed food	Protein (g)	Fat (g)	Carbo-hydrates (g)	Na (mg)	K (mg)	Ca (mg)	P (mg)	Fe (IU)
Carrot	1.0	0.2	7.3	45	280	35	30	0.7
Corn salad	1.8	0.4	2.6	4	420	30	50	2.0
Endive	1.7	0.2	2.0	50	350	50	50	1.4
Lettuce	1.2	0.2	1.7	8	220	20	35	0.6
Parsley	4.4	0.4	9.8	30	1,000	240	130	8.0
Radish	1.0	0.1	3.5	17	255	34	26	1.5
Red beet	1.5	0.1	7.6	86	340	30	45	0.9
Spinach	2.4	0.4	2.4	60	660	110	48	3.0

Average Composition of Some Commonly Used Seeds for Lovebirds

Seeds	Moisture (%)	Protein (%)	Fat (%)	Fiber (%)	Ca (%)	P (%)	Ash (%)	Carbo-hydrates (%)
Common millet (*Panicum millaceum*)	9.2	13.1	3.3	9.1	0.03	0.4	4.1	59.7
Spray millet (*Setaria italica*)	12.5	15.0	6.1	11.2	0.03	0.32	6.0	60.1
Canary grass seed (*Phalaris canariensis*)	15.1	13.7	4.1	21.3	0.05	0.55	10.0	56.2
Hullet oats (*Avena sativa*)	10.0	12.1	4.4	12.0	0.09	0.33	3.4	64.3
Niger seed (*Guizotia abyssinica*)	7.0	20.0	43.2	14.3	0.43	0.65	3.5	12
Flax seed (*Linum usitatissimum*)	7.1	24.2	37.0	6.3	0.23	0.66	4.1	20
Sunflower seed (*Helianthus annuus*)	7.1	15.2	28.3	29.1	0.18	0.45	3.2	17.5
Milo (*Andropogon sorghum*)	12.5	12.1	3.6	2.4	0.03	0.27	1.9	69
Safflower (*Carthamus tinctorius*)	7.2	14.3	28.0	31.2	–	–	3.0	16.5

Vitamin A (IU)	Vitamin B$_1$ (mg)	Vitamin B$_2$ (mg)	Vitamin C (mg)
13,500	70	55	6
7,000	65	80	30
900	52	120	9
1,500	60	90	10
12,080	140	300	170
38	33	30	30
80	22	40	10
8,200	86	240	47

for your lovebird. As a general rule, the answer is "no." If your bird has a healthy diet that includes a quality seed mix variety of yellow and dark green leafy vegetables, then your bird is probably already eating a healthy diet. Powdered vitamins that you sprinkle on top of the food simply get filtered down through the seeds to the bottom of the dish where they get buried under the chaff and are not eaten. Liquid vitamins added to the water supply encourage the growth of potentially harmful bacteria, and therefore increase the odds of your bird becoming ill.

In the event that your avian veterinarian recommends that your bird be given a vitamin

supplement because it is a fussy eater and doesn't eat its vegetables, the best way to get them into the bird is by sprinkling them onto a "heat and eat"-style food, because the powder sticks to the moist food and is more likely to be ingested.

BRINGING YOUR LOVEBIRD HOME

Although it is possible that there may be circumstances where you unexpectedly find yourself as caretaker of a strange lovebird (finding a lost one, inheriting one when your children go off to college, or getting one through the illness/death of the previous owner), if at all possible you should try to be as fussy as you can about the quality and personality of the bird you acquire.

Are You Ready?

You've read the books, bought the supplies, and are ready to take the plunge. Now what?

There are several possible sources for lovebirds: pet stores, breeders, animal shelters, and ads in the local paper, but each source needs to be viewed critically. You want a pet with whom you can interact, and not just a colorful decorative accessory. The best thing you can do is to find a healthy, well-socialized specimen from a reliable source to get your owner-pet relationship off to the best start possible.

Before you go to choose your bird, make sure that you are ready.

Even a small bird requires a large commitment.

✔ Read this book and others like it, so that you are an informed consumer. Birds are about the worst impulse buy that a person can make, and if a person is not going to be able to meet all of the bird's social, emotional, and physical needs, then it's not fair to the bird to be brought into their home.

✔ Make sure that the cage and supplies are purchased and set up before you buy the bird, so that its new home is ready when it gets there, rather than having the bird sit afraid in a dark box for an extended period of time while waiting for the owner to finish setting up.

✔ If you have other birds or pets in the house, make sure that the cage is set up in a different part of the house; new birds should always be quarantined, both to make sure that they don't carry illnesses that could affect your resident birds and to give them time to settle into their new cages before they are confronted with their first view of the family dog or cat.

Your New Bird

Before you bring your new bird home, make sure that everything is prepared: that the cage is set up, that you have a supply of food ready, and you have all of the information that you need to provide it with a proper home. It's a good idea to make an appointment with an avian veterinarian for a "new bird checkup" even before you get the bird, perhaps even

arranging it so that you stop at the clinic or office on the way home. If there is a health problem, the sooner you detect it, the easier it is to enforce whatever guarantee the bird came with, and if you need to return the bird, it is much easier to do so before you get to know it and become attached.

Pet Stores

Pet stores are very convenient; most areas have one. But they vary widely in terms of the quality of the animals, the care with which the animals are provided, and the competence and knowledge of the staff.

Appearances can tell you quite a bit. Visit the store several times before you make the decision to patronize it.

✔ Do the animals all look healthy?

✔ Are the cages clean, and the dishes of food and water always clean and full?

✔ Do the birds have a supply of toys in the cages to play with, or are they required to spend their time sitting there with nothing to do but eat and watch the people go by?

✔ Are there mineral blocks and cuttlebones provided?

✔ Was the mistake made of offering the birds grit?

The above list contains all the signs that will tell you if the birds in the store are well cared for or not.

Don't give in to buying a bird from a disreputable pet store in order to "rescue" it; the odds are that such a bird would be sick before you ever purchased it, creating unnecessary expenses and potential heartache for you, and the store would merely replace the bird with another that would be subjected to the same

═══ CHECKLIST ═══

Questions for the Breeder

1 Ask the breeder what species they breed and how often.

2 Does the breeder pull his or her chicks to be handfed? (Most breeders will leave the chicks with their parents for the first couple of weeks, then pull them after the babies are able to go through the night without a feeding.)

3 What sort of diet does the breeder feed the birds?

4 Does the breeder handle the babies to get them used to people?

5 Does the breeder offer any sort of guarantee?

6 Can you call the breeder after the purchase if you have any questions?

A young white masked lovebird. Never bring home a bird that isn't fully weaned.

treatment. If you are unfortunate enough to come across a store where the cages are dirty and the birds look ill or unkempt, tactfully explain to the clerk what you see as a problem, and then make sure that they know why you will not be buying a bird from that store. Such places don't care about the animals they sell as much as about the money that they can make, and the best way to get them to "shape up" is to make them realize that they are losing money by their unkind practices.

Before you purchase a bird, ask the clerk if you can handle it first. The best pets are the ones that are already tame and are not afraid of hands or handling. If the lovebirds are not tame, watch out! Their beaks may be small, but they can still leave a bruise or even draw blood. Although lovebirds can be tamed even if they were not hand-raised, it is probably worth your while to keep looking until you find a bird that is ready to be an interactive pet.

Breeders

Many people prefer to buy their birds directly from the breeder. Breeders can be found through classified ads in bird magazines and on the Internet. When you first contact a breeder, ask questions to find out about their breeding operation and how much they know about a species. Don't be surprised if a breeder interviews you at the same time; most reputable breeders want their birds to go to good homes, and they'll want to make sure that you are well informed before you decide to buy one of their birds.

The ideal breeder will answer all your questions and even have a few for you. He or she will have happy, healthy, fully weaned babies ready to go (never buy an unweaned baby bird; handfeeding is not child's play and an amateur can make mistakes that are painful at the very least and fatal at the very worst). If he or she sells unweaned babies, look elsewhere. Some breeders will invite you in to see their operation while others will ask you to wait in one room while they get the baby and bring it to you—both are acceptable. In some places birds are often stolen and so the breeders would prefer not to let outsiders know what kinds of birds they have on the premises. Reputable breeders will introduce you to the babies they have available, and may even steer you toward a particular one if he or she thinks that that bird's temperament meets your particular needs.

Because breeders sell the birds directly to the consumer, they are usually less expensive than pet stores.

Choosing a single lovebird can be a daunting task.

Secondhand Birds

Great caution should be used if you are thinking of acquiring a secondhand bird, whether it is through an animal shelter, an ad in the paper, or an acquaintance. With a secondhand bird, you not only get the bird, but also all of the health, behavioral, and emotional issues that come with it. You risk large veterinary bills, bloody fingers, and an uphill battle in forming an owner-pet bond.

The first thing to ask when considering a secondhand bird is why the bird is up for adoption. It may be a perfectly legitimate reason, such as the fact that it was a recaptured lost bird whose owner cannot be found; the original owner may have died or become unable to care for it; or the owner is forced to give up the bird due to an unforeseen move.

It's also possible that the bird is available because the owner tired of it, or that something about the bird's behavior irritated the owner to the point where he or she no longer wanted the bird. If one of these is the case, proceed with caution. You want a bird you can interact with and handle. A bird that was neglected is less likely to be hand-tame and more likely to be aggressive about defending its territory within the cage.

Behavior

A bird that is being given up for behavioral reasons should be considered with great caution. Observe the bird for yourself. If the owner complains about the noise, visit the bird yourself and see if you find it excessively noisy. If he or she wants to give up the bird because it bites, are you willing to be bitten while you work to correct that behavior? If he or she wants to give the bird up because "it just sits there," observe the bird carefully to look for signs of illness: is it sitting upright and erect on the perch, or is it huddled on the floor? This is a clear sign of a sick bird.

A secondhand bird that is being given up because of behavior or neglect is not a hopeless case. Even a bird that has been abused has the potential to be redeemed. One of my cockatiels came from a home where the children yelled at him and shook his cage. He drew blood the first time I met him, but now acts as if the sun rises every time I walk into the room and he can't get to perch on my hand fast enough. However, with any secondhand pet, it will probably be a long, arduous battle to gain its health and its trust, with no guarantee of success.

Illness

A bird that shows signs of illness is best avoided, no matter how sorry you feel for it. Even if the bird is free, you can easily spend hundreds on veterinarian bills and medications for it, and the bird may develop a permanent grudge against you if you have to catch it and force it to swallow nasty-tasting medicine

Look for a bird that will interact with people.

several times a day. If you have other birds, it could possibly infect them as well.

Secondhand birds can turn out to be lovely, affectionate pets, but they can also turn out to be an emotional disaster. Proceed with caution.

Picking Out Your Bird

There are several factors that will go into deciding which lovebird you will ultimately take home. Sometimes it's simply a matter of availability, and what birds you can find in your area when you go looking. Other people will be taken with the appearance of a particular species of lovebird and will actively look online and in stores and advertisements for tame babies of that particular species. And a lucky few will encounter an individual bird that takes an instant liking to them and with whom they feel an instant connection—for

Signs of a Healthy Lovebird

✔ Sits high on the perch.
✔ Seems as curious about you as you are about it.
✔ Has smooth, unpuffed feathers.
✔ Eyes are open and clear.
✔ No nasal discharge.
✔ Has a stocky, well-filled-out build.
✔ Does not sneeze or cough.
✔ Has droppings that are solid, green to greenish-brown and white, and not runny or wet.

them, it doesn't matter what the bird's age or gender or species is; they have found the bird they were meant to have.

When you have found a place that has lovebirds available and that you feel comfortable buying a bird from, you may have to decide among several different babies. Beyond assuring yourself that they are healthy and well socialized, there really is no right or wrong way to choose. You can make your decision based on appearance, personality, individual appeal, or an arbitrary factor such as hatch date or the way an individual waggles its tail every time you pick it up. My own peach-faced lovebird, Doodle, was picked because she hatched on December 31, 1999, making her the last lovebird of the 1900s.

It's worth the extra time and effort to find a place that sells babies that were hand-raised, even though they will likely charge more for those babies. It's a better investment to purchase a bird that is already accustomed to being handled; then you can begin with a bird that enjoys people rather than one that fears them. A well-socialized baby lovebird should

step onto your hand willingly, and let you handle it without it trying to bite or flee.

Under no circumstances should you buy a bird that is not able to eat on its own. Hand-feeding can be a very risky proposition, and as stated earlier can easily result in the death of the bird. If someone tries to sell you an unweaned baby, do not buy it—go elsewhere to find your bird. Such a suggestion tells you that either the person does not know what he or she is talking about, or that he or she is more interested in a quick buck than the health and well-being of the birds.

Try to pick a bird that seems comfortable with you. Blink at it and see if it blinks back. Handle it, talk to it, and offer to scratch its head. If a bird seems reluctant to interact with you, put it down and try a cagemate instead. Sometimes it's easier to eliminate the birds you don't want than to discover the one that you do. And if none of the birds grab your fancy, don't be afraid to decline them all and wait for another day.

You want a lovebird that will be an interactive companion, a relationship that will last for years. The easiest way to do that is to start off by liking each other.

Getting Settled

Once you get the bird home, place it gently inside its new cage and shut the door. Give the bird 24 to 48 hours to acclimate to its new home, letting it explore the interior of its cage and observe the comings and goings of the household.

It's very important to keep the bird away from any other pet birds you might own for at least the first 30 days, even if the initial veterinary visit finds no problems. The bird may have been exposed to illnesses that require a period of incubation before symptoms begin to appear, and it is much easier to keep the birds separated at first than to risk spreading any illnesses to your own birds.

While you are observing this quarantine, tend to your resident bird before you take care of the new bird so that you don't inadvertently carry any germs from the newcomer back to the resident bird. Wash thoroughly with soap every time you finish handling the new bird to kill any germs that you might have picked up from it.

The Veterinary Checkup

It's important to have a good relationship with your veterinarian. You need one who is not only an experienced avian veterinarian, but one with whom you feel comfortable. Bringing your bird to the veterinarian for a checkup as soon as possible after you buy it is important, not just for the peace of mind that it will give you, but also because checking the bird when it is healthy allows the veterinarian to find out exactly what is "normal" for your bird and to advise you about any particular needs your bird may have. If your bird's wings were not clipped when you brought it home, the veterinarian can clip them for you and/or show you how to do the job yourself. If you are really curious whether your bird is a male or a female and would like to know the answer before you assign it a name, you can also ask your veterinarian to perform DNA sexing, which determines gender using a small sample of blood or a freshly plucked chest feather.

Visit your veterinarian for a well-bird visit.

A well-bird visit will begin with the veterinarian asking what you know about the bird—how old it is, how long you have had it, etc. A good veterinarian will not only check to make sure that the bird is healthy, but will check to make sure that you know how to keep it that way. Listen to whatever advice you are given; both you and your bird will benefit if you do. The veterinarian will check the bird's overall health, examining the eyes, the nares (nostrils), and feathers, looking inside the mouth, weighing the bird, and observing whatever droppings are present.

The individual tests that a veterinarian performs on your bird depend, to some extent, on what is already known about your bird's history. Generally, the veterinarian will draw a blood sample to check whether or not your bird has an elevated white blood cell count, a sign of infection or illness. He or she may take swabs from inside the bird's mouth and vent area to look for the presence of harmful bacteria or fungus.

Do not be surprised if this initial visit costs more than the bird itself, but consider it an investment in a long and healthy relationship.

LIVING WITH LOVEBIRDS

The key to fostering a good relationship with your bird is consistency. A bird that knows what to expect is a happy, secure individual. Make certain to have a designated amount of quality time to interact with your bird every day in order to maintain that bond.

Handling Your Lovebird

Assuming that your lovebird is tame, you should be able to get it to step onto your hand by gently nudging its lower chest with your finger and saying *"Up"* (you can ask the pet store or breeder what specific word they used; the words themselves are not as important as the tone of voice and the nudging finger). The bird should step obligingly onto your finger. The proper way to hold your hand is with the index finger up toward the ceiling and the other fingers curled into your palm. Here are some other pointers:

✔ Some lovebirds become very territorial about their cages and may try to bite your hand when you reach into the cage, but will step onto your hand willingly if you approach them when they are away from it. In this case, you can try to use a wooden dowel rather than

Lovebirds make a lively addition to any household.

your hand to have them step onto and remove them from the cage that way.

✔ Once you have the lovebird out of the cage, move steadily and try to avoid making fast, jerking motions. Lovebirds have strong feet and can hold on quite firmly, but any jarring motions may be upsetting to the bird.

✔ Do not try to pet your bird on the back as you would a cat or a dog. Lovebirds don't like this, and for a very good reason. In the wild, if a predator is going to catch a lovebird, it does so by reaching down from above the bird and over its back, pinning its wings to its sides and making flight impossible. When you try to pet a lovebird's back, it's the same sort of approach that a wild animal would make if it were planning to make a meal out of the love-bird; consequently, being touched on the back is a sensation that few lovebirds will tolerate.

✔ The best way to physically interact with a lovebird is to touch it in a way that resembles how one lovebird would touch another. Love-

A lovebird will twist itself into a variety of positions in an effort to preen, but needs help to preen its head and neck.

birds cannot reach their heads and the backs of their necks, so they are dependent on other lovebirds to take care of these areas for them. Not only do lovebirds clean each other's feathers, but they also help to break open the shafts of the new feather as they come in.

Preening

To make your lovebird really feel good, try scratching it on the head, under the beak, on the cheeks, and on the back of the neck. If you feel any short, pointed quills poking through, these are the new feathers that are coming in. Gently squeeze or scratch the sides of these feathers so that the waxy casing falls away and the barbules of the feathers break free. Incoming feathers can be itchy, so most birds thoroughly enjoy this process, although, if you try to remove the casing too close to the skin,

the bird will feel this as a pinch and may emit a loud squeak accompanied by a peck. This is the bird's way of telling you to be a little more careful. It does not mean, however, that it wants you to stop, and most birds will immediately lower their heads, inviting you to return to the job of helping them preen.

Lovebirds may also be the ones to initiate these preening sessions by lowering their heads toward the floor to show you that they want their heads and necks scratched. It is also not unusual for your lovebird to want to preen you in return, carefully nibbling your skin or hair. This is fine, but if the nibbling becomes too rough, let the bird know immediately by telling it *"No!"* in a firm voice and giving it the same kind of look that your third-grade teacher gave you when she didn't approve of what you were doing. A second hard nibble should result in the bird being immediately returned to the cage, ending your interactions until it can behave like a gentle, well-mannered bird once again.

Taming

Taming a lovebird is not an easy undertaking. It does not trust people and is not afraid to bite in the interest of what it views as self-defense.

If you acquire an untamed lovebird and want to try to tame it, be prepared to gain ground slowly and go through lots of

Lovebirds kept in pairs spend much of their time preening each other.

Band-Aids in the process. Having the bird's wings clipped will make the job much easier because the bird won't be able to fly off as easily and will be easier to recapture if it does. (For more on clipping, see our special "How-To" section on page 58.)

Blinking: Begin outside the cage, sitting quietly near the bird without directly looking at it to accustom it to your presence. Reading near the bird's cage is a good way to let the bird observe you without feeling threatened. When the bird no longer flutters and tries to flee when you near the cage, try blinking your eyes at it in an obvious manner—in the wild, a predator that is stalking a lovebird will stare at it unceasingly. Blinking signals to the bird that you are not stalking it, and many lovebirds will blink back in response.

Food treats: Once the bird seems comfortable with your presence, try reaching into the cage with a special food treat in the palm of your hand. A good time to do this is first thing in the morning before you feed the bird. Rest your hand with the treat palm up on the bottom of the cage and wait to see if the bird will land on your hand. Try not to react or to remove your hand quickly if the bird attacks it; doing so would teach your bird that it can get you out of its cage by biting you, and that's not a good lesson to be learned. You can pick up a book and read it while the bird looks at and considers the treat. If, after a while, there has been no advance on the part of the bird to perch on your hand and eat, place the treat in the dish and remove your hand. The best treats are foods that your bird likes but does not get as an ordinary part of its diet, such as a fresh

A split-albino masked lovebird.

vegetable (corn seems to be a particular favorite), a fig, or an almond.

Eating off your palm: Once the bird begins to land on your hand, spend the next few days just letting it eat off your palm inside the

Introducing a second lovebird is most likely to be successful if the new bird is of the same species.

below: An untamed lovebird will retreat to the farthest corners of the cage the first time you reach for it.

cage. Gradually move your hand closer to the door. Finally, try to remove the bird from the cage while it is still eating on your hand. This is not going to be an easy task, and the bird may hop off your hand many times before you can get it to come out of the cage.

Touching: Once you can manage to get the bird on your hand and out of the cage, praise it profusely and blink at it to reassure it that it's not in any danger. See if you can get it to stay perched even after the food has been eaten. When the bird seems fairly comfortable with you, slowly raise your free hand and see if it will let you rub its face and scratch its neck and chin. Once the bird lets you touch it this way, it is pretty much tame. From here, you need to teach the bird to step up on your finger by gently nudging it on the chest and saying *"Up"* (or whatever words you choose). Praise the bird enthusiastically whenever you succeed in getting it to follow this simple, but very important, command.

Second Birds

Many people start off with a single bird and develop a warm, happy relationship with it, then they feel guilty because they have to work and are gone all day. They worry that their bird is lonely or bored while they are gone and they start to wonder if they should get a second bird as a companion for the first one.

The answer for many lovebird owners is "No." If you have a pet that is friendly and affectionate, introducing a second lovebird may jeopardize your relationship. It may well form a bond with the second bird and focus all of its time and affection on the other bird rather than on you. It may even feel the need to defend its new friend from you, and it will begin to bite. It is also possible that if you have two lovebirds, you will end up with a pair that mate and produce young, presenting you with a whole new set of challenges that you don't necessarily want. Also, your lovebird may act very aggressively toward the newcomer.

Lovebirds are very territorial and are apt to attack a nonlovebird without regard to the difference in size. This can result in either or both being injured. For this reason, introducing a nonlovebird as a second bird is not recommended.

If you already own a bird other than a lovebird and want to add a lovebird as a second bird, the chances are good that the lovebird will make a power play and attack the resident bird every chance it gets. While they may be good as single pets, lovebirds, in general, really do not do well as second birds outside of their species.

There are exceptions, of course. On occasion, a lovebird will take a fancy to a second bird and will get along well with it, but as a general rule, lovebirds are too aggressive to safely introduce a companion.

If you truly feel that something in their lives is missing and that your bird really needs a feathered companion, even if it means that your owner-pet relationship may suffer because of it, then the best choice is to get a second lovebird of the same species. Peach-faced hens seem to be the least welcoming of newcomers. Newcomers should be younger than the resident bird, and they should be introduced gradually. The new bird must be kept quarantined away from the resident bird for at least 30 days to avoid the risk of spreading a contagious illness. You can use this quarantine period to begin to form a bond with the new bird, but after each encounter be sure to wash thoroughly before you go in to handle your resident bird.

Introducing the Birds

When the birds are finally introduced, they should be kept in separate cages across the room from each other for at least two weeks in order to give them a chance to safely observe and get used to each other. To avoid jealousy issues, always attend to your first bird before the newcomer; go to it first, talk to it first, feed it first, and take it out first. It expects to be your number one; the newcomer doesn't.

Putting the Birds Together

When it's time to put both birds together, begin by letting them "out" at the same time;

TIP

this gives the newer bird plenty of room to flee if the need arises. When you put the birds in a common cage, put them in a third cage, one that neither has occupied, to avoid the situation where one feels that the other is invading its territory. Provide extra dishes so that who gets to eat first is not an issue, and observe them carefully. With luck, the birds will form a deep and affectionate bond.

Bathing

Almost all species of lovebirds in the wild live close to the water, not just for drinking, but also for bathing. Wild lovebirds love to bathe and will stand in the shallows, splashing and soaking themselves in a way that looks like the bird is having great fun.

In captivity, it's still important that birds be allowed to bathe to maintain skin and feather health. There are special "birdbaths" available in pet stores for birds, but I find that a pie plate filled with room-temperature water works just as well. If a bird seems reluctant to bathe, you can encourage it by splashing in the water with your fingers yourself. Be prepared for the entire area to get wet, because an enthusiastic bather will also soak the surrounding area with its splashing.

If your bird still does not seem to want to bathe (and many birds will bathe on their own in their water dishes when you may not be looking), a weekly spraying with a plant mister may be in order. Try spraying upward so that the mist falls down on the bird like a gentle rain rather than spraying at it directly.

Vacations

No matter how much you love your bird, there will be times when you need to be away from it, either for business or personal reasons. Lovebirds are very social beings and cannot be happy if they are simply left well stocked with food in an empty cage for days at a time. There are several options available. You can either send the bird, cage and all, on a "vaca-

Most lovebirds enjoy bathing, either in shallow water or under a gentle spray.

If a bird needs to be restrained when clipping its nails, hold the head and beak with the thumb and index finger to avoid being bit.

tion" of its own to the house of a bird-friendly acquaintance, hire someone to come in and feed the bird in your absence, or send the bird to a boarding facility. If you choose the last option, you should use the same criteria that you used when deciding where to buy your bird. If you would not buy a bird from a particular store, then don't board your bird there.

Sending a bird to the home of a friend or having a friend come into your house to feed and visit with it reduces the risk of exposing it to other birds that may have contagious diseases. No matter which option you choose, try to keep the bird in its own cage with its own toys and the food that it's accustomed to, so that it will be as comfortable as possible.

Nail Trimming

For the most part, lovebirds will wear their nails down through their daily activities. However, if you find that your bird's nails are catching on cloth, rug, toys, or perch, or if the nails are becoming too long and sharp for you to hold the bird comfortably, you may want to trim its nails. Because a bird's nails, like its blood feathers, have blood vessels inside them, you need to be careful when trimming them. Have someone else restrain the bird and hold it up to the light so that you can see the thin line that runs through the middle of the nail;

Be sure not to cut into the part with blood vessels. The illustration on the right shows the proper way to clip nails.

that is the blood vessel and you want to cut below it at approximately a 45-degree angle. I use a baby's nail clipper for this job because it's easier to see and maneuver than an adult-sized clipper.

If you accidentally cut the nail too short, you can use a styptic stick (available at a pet store) or cornstarch to help stop the bleeding and promote clotting. If this is the case, stop the nail-trimming session and return the bird to its cage rather than stress the bird further.

Beak Trimming

A normal, healthy lovebird has a fairly long beak that should keep itself worn down through normal daily use. It should never need to be trimmed. Excessive beak growth is a sign of a metabolic disorder, such as liver disease, and a veterinarian should be consulted to diagnose the condition and trim back the excess beak. This is not a job for an amateur to attempt.

LOVEBIRD SPECIES

Of the nine known subspecies of lovebird, three—the peach-faced, masked, and Fischer's—are commonly available as pets. These three come in a wide variety of colors and mutations, and the one you choose may depend on availability, appearance, or the personality of an individual bird.

Peach-faced Lovebirds

Scientific name: *Agapornis roseicollis roseicollis*

First scientific record: In 1817 by Louis Jean Pierre Vieillot

Appearance: Peach-faced lovebirds are bright, apple-green-colored birds whose undersides are somewhat lighter than their backs. Their faces and bibs are, as the name implies, an orange-peach color. Their rumps are a bright sky blue and their tails have bands of bright blue, orange, and green. Their beaks are a yellowy horn color and their feet are gray.

There is a hint of white eye rings surrounding their brown eyes, but these are not as prominent as they are in the masked lovebird. Females and young peach-faced lovebirds may

A lutino peach-faced lovebird.

be a little duller-colored than the males, but there is really no dependable way to visually tell the males from the females. Young lovebirds may have less peach coloring on their foreheads and some black on their beaks, but this will change as the bird matures. At 6 to 7 inches (15–18 cm) long, peach-faced lovebirds are often the biggest (but not the heaviest) of the nine lovebird species, although the difference between the species is less than an inch and a half (3.75 cm). Peach-faced females tend to be slightly larger than the males.

Habitat: In the wild, peach-faced lovebirds live in the southwest portion of Africa, living in coastal plains or in dry plains near mountains in Namibia and southwestern Angola. They live in fairly small groups and are always found close to a source of water. They live on a diet of seeds and berries, and have the unfortunate habit of helping themselves to area crops.

A Quick Guide to Lovebird Mutations

Ino: An "ino" is a genetic mutation in which the bird lacks a particular pigment that is found in the wild species. This is similar to albinos in humans and other animals, but in birds, they can be missing one pigment but have others. A normally green bird that is lacking in blue pigment, for example, would appear yellow, because the yellow and the blue together make green.

Because inos lack the pigment combination needed to make the black pigment that normally lines the inside of the eye and absorbs light as it passes through the eye to the brain, they are particularly light-sensitive and are most comfortable in rooms with indirect or lower wattage lighting.

The two most common forms of ino mutation are the creamino (which is similar to an albino and is missing most of the pigments, resulting in a bright white or cream-colored bird) and the lutino, which lacks blue pigment and thus looks like a bright yellow bird with red eyes (although features that don't contain the blue pigment will not be changed in appearance, so a lutino peach-faced lovebird, for example, would have a bright yellow body and a peach face because the face does not normally contain any blue pigment).

Ino is a recessive, sex-linked trait, which means that it has to be passed down from both parents (although you can have a bird that carries the ino gene but looks like a typical member of the species).

Pied: A pied bird is one whose colors appear in patches, rather than solid colors.

Dilute: A lighter-colored version of the original appearance.

Cinnamon: A form of ino mutation in which the black pigments are replaced with brown, giving the bird softer-looking colors.

Dark Factors: When the birds colors appear darker than the normal members of the species because of the way light is reflected by the feathers.

Pet potential: Peach-faced lovebirds are the most common of all lovebirds available as pets because of their hardy constitution and the ease with which they breed in captivity. Although they—particularly the hens—have a reputation for being temperamental and feisty, a handfed, well-socialized peach-faced lovebird can make an excellent pet.

Mutations: There is a wide variety of color variations in captive-bred peach-faced lovebirds—and not all of them have peach-colored faces! The most common mutation is called "pied." A pied bird is one with a genetic mutation that has distinct patches of color on its body rather than being the solid green of the wild type of peach-faced lovebird. Most common is a variety that has patches of green and yellow, although patches of greenish blue are also possible. In some birds, the patches of green are so small that the bird is predominantly yellow or blue-green. Baby pieds lack the black markings on the beak that other peach-faced lovebirds have, alerting the breeder that the baby will be special-looking even before it has its feathers!

A normal masked lovebird and a blue mutation of the same species.

Masked Lovebirds

Scientific name: *Agapornis personata personata*

First scientific record: In 1887 by Anton Reichenow

Description: Wild masked lovebirds have bright green and a dark brown to black head with a bright yellow collar and bib. The covert feathers on the tail are green with a faint bluish tinge to them. Their eyes are brown and the area around the eye is without feathers, resulting in a large ring of white flesh around the eye. Their beaks are a deep, vibrant red and their feet are gray. There's no way to visually

tell a male from a female, although the young masked lovebirds are noticeably duller-colored than their parents.

Habitat: Masked lovebirds are native to a small area in northeastern Tanzania. They are described as nomadic, live in flocks, brood in colonies, and nest in tree hollows, although there are also reports of them taking over the abandoned nests of other types of birds. They will also nest in nooks and crannies of buildings if given the opportunity, and have a reputation for being particularly destructive in fields of millet and corn.

Pet potential: Masked lovebirds are the second most popular and readily available of the pet lovebirds.

Mutations: The most common mutation of masked lovebird is the blue masked, which shares the blackish mask of the normal version, but has a blue body instead of a green one with grayish white in place of the bright yellow and a pale pink beak.

Fischer's Lovebirds

Scientific name: *Agapornis fischeri*
First scientific record: Discovered by Anton Reichenow in 1887
Description: Fischer's lovebirds have green backs, wings, and chests with an orange face and a yellow-orange neck. Their beaks are red, their tails are green with sky-blue tips, and their eyes are surrounded by a featherless

opposite page: Variations on a peach-faced theme.

Clockwise from top left: normal, creamino, lutino, pied.

ring of white skin. Males and females are identical, and young Fischer's look like more dully colored versions of their parents except that they often have dark-colored markings at the base of their beaks that fade as they mature.

Habitat: When they are not in breeding season, indigenous Fischer's lovebirds live in flocks of 20 to 80 birds in the trees and thorn bushes of savannahs to the south and southeast of Lake Victoria in Tanzania. They are often heard before they are seen and are not shy, helping themselves to crops of millet, grain, and corn, feeding on the ground in groups of up to several hundred birds. They are nomadic, and probably have seasonal migration patterns. There are reports of them being seen in high elevations, as much as 5,000 feet (1,500 m) above sea level.

Pet potential: Although not as common as the peach-faced and masked lovebirds, Fischer's are regularly available as pets. They tend to be slightly smaller than masked lovebirds, while their call is generally louder and higher pitched. They are also somewhat more difficult to find available for sale and consequently may be higher priced, although they breed well in captivity and are becoming increasingly more available as pets. They have a reputation for being less feisty than some of the other species, and can make charming and highly interactive pets.

Mutations: Fischer's come in a blue mutation, as well as lutino and albino. Dilute versions, whose colors are not as dark as those of the wild variety, are also available. Other mutations are reportedly being achieved by breeders, but are not yet generally available as pets.

The remaining six species of lovebirds are much more rare and are not likely to be available as pets:

Black-cheeked Lovebirds

Scientific name: *Agapornis personata nigrigenis*

First scientific record: Discovered by William Lutley Sclater in 1906

Description: Wild black-cheeked lovebirds look very similar to black masked lovebirds, but the area of yellow is much more orange-green and is limited to the bird's throat rather than extending down the chest and around the back of the neck. The area of dark brown-black does not extend to the crown of the head as it does on the masked lovebird. Their beaks are red, their tails are green, and they have white eye rings.

Because of their similarities, many people have paired black-cheeked lovebirds with masked lovebirds and produced hybridized young that fall into neither category. This is particularly unfortunate because the black-cheeked is considered to be very endangered in the wild. Female black-cheeked lovebirds resemble the males, as do the young, which may also have black near the base of their beaks.

Habitat: Black-cheeked lovebirds have a very limited range in the wild, and are found only in the Zambezi River Valley of Zambia, where they inhabit lowlands and woodlands. It is estimated that the entire wild population of black-cheeked lovebirds live in an area of just 80 square miles (129 km).

Pet potential: Because purebred individuals of these birds are so rare at this time, they should not be kept as pets, but should be restricted to breeding situations where they are paired only with other birds of the same species.

Mutation: There are reports of both a blue and a yellow mutation among black-cheeked lovebirds, but it is difficult to be sure that these are "pure" black-cheeked birds and not the result of hybridization with masked lovebird mutations.

Nyasa Lovebirds

Scientific name: *Agapornis lilianae*

First scientific record: Discovered by George Ernest Shelley in 1894

Description: Nyasas have a bright green body and wings, with a lighter shade of green on the belly. Their foreheads and crown are a reddish orange that fades to more of a coral color on their cheeks and throat. The female is identical to the male, although her feathers and eyes may be a little lighter, and the female is often smaller. Their tails are the same green as their wings and back, ending in a reddish orange tip. Their beaks are red and they have brown eyes surrounded by a white eye ring. Young Nyasas are less brightly colored and the color in their cheeks is somewhat less pronounced. At about 5½ inches (13.9 cm), Nyasas are the smallest of the eye ring group of lovebirds.

Habitat: Wild Nyasas live in river valleys in Zimbabwe, eastern Malawi, southeastern Tanzania, and northwestern Mozambique. Nyasas live in close proximity to water and have been reported at elevations as high as 5,000 feet (1,500 m) above sea level. They normally travel in flocks of 30 to 40 birds and breed in colonies. Unlike other lovebird species that transport nesting material by weaving it through their feathers, Nyasas carry nesting material in their beaks. Nyasa lovebirds get their name from their natural territory; until 1964, Malawi was a British colony known as "Nyasaland."

Pet potential: Nyasa are relatively rare in captivity and are not usually kept as pets, although there are reports of increased success in their captive breeding.

Mutations: The most common mutation of the Nyasa lovebird is the lutino, which appears as a yellow bird with a red head and eyes. There are also reports of a blue mutation, but this is very rare.

Abyssinian Lovebirds (also called Black-winged Lovebirds)

Scientific name: *Agapornis taranta taranta*
First scientific record: Discovered by Stanley in 1814

Description: Abyssinians are one of the few species of lovebird that is sexually dimorphic; that is, the males look different from the females. Male Abyssinians have a small red or gray eye ring and a patch of red on the forehead; the female has no such red. Both have a green body, green tail, red beak, and black underwing covert and flight feathers, which give the species its alternative name. Young Abyssinians resemble the females, although their colors are somewhat duller than those of the adults and their beaks are a brownish yellow for the first few weeks of their lives. Although peach-faced lovebirds are the longest of the lovebird species, the Abyssinians are generally the heaviest.

Habitat: Abyssinians are native to the mountain forests of Ethiopia, a country that in ancient times was known as "Abyssinia," from which the species takes its name. They are found at elevations of up to 10,000 feet (3,000 m). Abyssinians live in small groups of 8 to 20 birds. They tend to return to the same tree night after night to roost, and therefore are more stationary than other lovebirds. They eat seeds with a high fat content and also berries and other fruits, particularly figs.

Pet potential: Abyssinians are not very common in captivity, and therefore are rarely available as pets. Males tend to be more interactive with people than females. Whereas other lovebirds chirp, Abyssinans have a rougher, more parrotlike call that they repeat rapidly while flying. Their diets in captivity should include figs, and young Abyssinians may also benefit from foods rich in vitamin C. Sprouted foods, such as millet, are also beneficial.

Mutations: The only reported color mutation of Abyssinian lovebirds is a single report of a cinnamon specimen.

Madagascar Lovebirds (also known as Gray-headed Lovebirds)

Scientific name: *Agapornis cana cana*
First scientific record: Discovered by Johan Gmelin in 1788

Description: Madagascar lovebirds are sexually dimorphic. Males have a green body, wings, and tail with a gray head, breast, and neck. The females resemble the males, but have no gray on the head, neck, and chest. Instead, they have yellow-green on the breast

and olive green on the sides of the face, crown, and back of the head. Young birds resemble the adults but with black at the base of their beak.

Habitat: Madagascar lovebirds take their name from the island nation of Madagascar, off the southeastern coast of Africa. They are found on the island of Madagascar and on many of the surrounding islands, such as Comoros, the Seychelles, and Mafia Islands. They are very shy in the wild and are reportedly heard more often than they are seen. When it's not mating season, they live in flocks of 5 to 20, although there are reports of them in flocks of up to 80 birds.

Pet potential: These birds are quite rare in captivity and are not available as pets. Birds kept in aviaries are reported to be flighty, shy, and sensitive to changes.

Mutations: There is no information available on any mutations of the Madagascar lovebird.

Red-faced Lovebirds

Scientific name: *Agaponris pullaria pullaria*
First scientific record: Attributed to Carolus Linnaeus in 1758

Description: Red-faced lovebirds have bright green backs, wings, and tails with lighter, yellow-green on their chests and bellies. The males have a red face and forehead while those of the females are a lighter reddish orange. The beaks are orange-red, with the male beak being

opposite page: Fischer's lovebirds.

left top: A normal peach-faced lovebird.

left bottom: The black-cheeked lovebird.

Comparing the Species

Species Name	Length	Sexually Dimorphic	Availability
Peach-faced *Agapornis roseicollis* (17 cm)	6.5 inches	No	Readily Available
Masked *A. personata* (15 cm)	6 inches	No	Readily Available
Fischer's *A. fischeri* (15 cm)	6 inches	No	Readily Available
Black-cheeked *A. nigrigenis* (13 cm)	5 inches	No	Difficult
Nyasa *A. lilianae* (13.5 cm)	5.5 inches	No	Difficult
Abyssinian *A. taranta* (17 cm)	6.5 inches	Yes	Difficult
Madagascar *A. cana* (14 cm)	5.5 inches	Yes	Difficult
Red-faced *A. pullaria* (15 cm)	6 inches	Yes	Difficult
Swindern's *A. Swindernia* (13 cm)	5 inches	No	Never kept in captivity

slightly darker than the female's. Young red-faced lovebirds resemble the adult females, but with a blackish base on the bill.

Habitat: Red-faced lovebirds are native to a wide area of central and central western Africa, including Guinea, Liberia, Ivory Coast, Ghana, Togo, Benin, Nigeria, Cameroon, Gabon, Congo, Northern Angola, the Central African Republic, Northern Zaire, Southern Sudan, Uganda, Rwanda, and Western Kenya. This is easily the largest range of any lovebird species, and helps to explain why they were the first lovebirds to be discovered by Western Europeans. They live in the trees in the lowlands, forests, and grasslands and return to the same roosting spots night after night. They normally live in small flocks of 15 to 20 birds but will congregate in huge flocks of several hundred when raiding agricultural fields of grain. They are reported to be very shy and unapproachable.

Pet potential: Red-faced lovebirds are very difficult to breed in captivity, therefore they are not available as pets. They are also reported to be very shy, nervous birds in the wild and thus would probably not do well as pets.

Mutations: There are no reported mutations of red-faced lovebirds.

Swindern's Lovebirds (also known as Black-collared Lovebirds)

Scientific name: *Agapornis swinderniana swinderniana*

First scientific record: Discovered by Heinrich Kuhl in 1820

Description: Swindern's have green bodies, wings, tail, and head, with a lighter green on the belly, a blue rump, and a curved black

Lutino peach-faced lovebird.

band that runs from the back of the neck all the way around the throat. Their beaks are grayish black. Females are believed to resemble the males; the young may be lacking the black "collar" before they mature.

Habitat: Swindern's lovebirds live in the forests of Liberia and Ghana, Cameroon, and central Zaire. Very little is known about wild Swindern's and they generally die within a few days in captivity. They are believed to eat seeds and grains, with figs as a vital part of their diet. There are also reports that they may eat insects.

Pet potential: There has never been a reported case of Swindern's being successfully bred in captivity, and wild-caught birds die soon after they are captured. There is only one reported case where Swindern's were kept alive for more than a few days, but this has never been duplicated.

Mutations: There are no known mutations of Swindern's lovebird.

SAFETY

Pet lovebirds are a lot like human toddlers. They are small, active, curious, and stubborn. These are all traits that may get them into trouble as they seek to explore things that are new to them.

Just as you need to "baby-proof" your house if you have a two-year-old child, you will also need to "bird-proof" your house if you are going to allow the bird out-of-cage time. We will try to cover some of the risks and hazards here and make suggestions as to what you can do to "bird-proof" your house.

To Clip or Not to Clip?

It's up to the individual owner to decide whether or not to clip (or have someone else clip) his or her bird's wings. Wing clipping is a bit of a misnomer; it's not the wing itself that gets cut, but rather, the long flight feathers at the end of the wing that the bird uses to gain altitude. Because there are no nerves in the feathers, cutting them midway causes the bird no more pain than a haircut or nail trim would cause you. And, like hair, the feathers eventually fall out and are replaced with new ones, so that

Take the proper steps to ensure the safety of your lovebird.

if you clip your bird's wing feathers today, they will be replaced by new, full-length feathers after a period of time, so that the wing clip does not permanently render the bird unable to fly.

A properly done wing clip does not "ground" the bird. The bird should be able to flap its wings and gain some forward motion, but without the long flight feathers, the bird can neither gain nor maintain any altitude. If a clipped bird should try to take off, instead of plummeting straight down like a rock, it will flutter a few feet forward as it falls, making for a gentler landing.

Advantages and Disadvantages

There are advantages and disadvantages to clipping a bird's wings. A bird that has been clipped is easier to handle and to tame than a bird that is able to fly. A clipped bird is also much less likely to get lost by flying out through an open door or window. Clipping reduces the dangers to the bird and to your belongings when your bird is outside the cage. Clipping also tends to curb a bird with a behavior problem. When my lovebird starts to get particularly nippy, we will clip her wings and find that she becomes much calmer and easy to handle afterward.

Disadvantages to clipping a bird's wings include the fact that if you have children or other pets in the house, it can be to the bird's benefit to be able to fly to avoid them. Some people also feel that it's unfair to clip the wings of a lovebird because it is part of their nature to be able to fly, and that flying provides a good opportunity to exercise. My own feeling is that each owner needs to weigh the risks in his or her particular situation, and then take whatever approach he or she feels is necessary to keep the bird as safe as possible.

Lost and Found Birds

It's very easy to lose a bird. All it takes is a careless moment—children running in and out, a friend at the door—and the bird can escape.

Although in some of the warmer places there are feral lovebirds that manage to band together and thrive, the odds are against a lovebird that escapes. Predators, inclement weather, cars, and lack of a safe food source may all doom a bird that gets lost.

Prevent Losing Your Bird

The best way to avoid this happening is by clipping the bird. A smart owner will also prepare in anticipation for such an emergency by taking a clear photo of the bird that can be used on a "Lost Bird" poster (if you have one of the common mutations, you may be able to get a usable picture of that species of lovebird from another source if you don't have one of your bird). Any identifying information, such as a leg band number, if there is one, should be written down and kept in a safe place. The owner should also try to make a recording of what the bird sounds like while it is happy and playing; if the bird does fly off, playing this recording loudly may help to guide it home, since it will seek out "other" lovebirds.

Action You Can Take

If your bird is lost, take immediate action.

1. Set its cage full of food outside with the door propped open so that it might see it and return.

2. Play the recording of lovebird sounds in case it's still in the area.

3. Call the newspaper, make posters, notify your local veterinarians and animal shelters and walk around your neighborhood, calling the bird or playing the recording in hopes of finding it. The more people you can make aware of the situation, the better the chances of recovering your bird.

4. Don't include the leg band number, if there is one, in your ads; save that for when the call comes that someone has found a lovebird to help prove that it is, indeed, your bird that they have.

Microchips

Some veterinarians will insert a tiny microchip under your bird's skin that can be used to identify it; this may be helpful if your bird was not banded as a chick. In some areas, local animal shelters have a scanner that will look for and read these chips, which will allow them to contact the owner and return the bird, but not all shelters have this technology, and it's up to you whether or not this would be a good option for your lovebird.

Household Dangers

There is a myth that birds are "low-maintenance" pets. This isn't exactly true. While you don't have to take them out in nasty weather to relieve themselves as you would a dog, and they don't demand that you get up to let them in and out like a cat, they still require daily feeding and watering and twice-weekly cage cleaning. Even a small bird can make a fairly big mess; seed husks, feathers, and shredded papers can all fall outside the cage and require daily vacuuming. Outside of the cage, lovebirds need constant supervision because their fearless curious natures can frequently put them at risk.

In the Kitchen

Kitchens are very dangerous places for birds, and are never suitable places for bird cages. Birds can fall into the sink, land on a hot stove (or worse, inside a hot pan), drown in a sink full of dishwater, and chew on electrical cords. These are all obvious dangers, but the single most dangerous thing in the kitchen for your bird is the one you probably don't recognize as a danger—nonstick pans.

The substance used in nonstick pans and cookware (such as Teflon, T-fal, or Silverstone) emits fumes at very high heat that irreversibly damage the bird's lungs. This damage quickly becomes fatal. The fumes, which are emitted by polytetrafluoroethylene (PTFE), the polymer

Some Plants That May Be Harmful to Your Lovebird

Avocado
Calla lily
English ivy
Hydrangea
Iris
Holly
Larkspur
Laurel
Mistletoe
Philodendron
Poinsettia

Some Plants That Are Safe for Your Lovebird

Aloe
African Violet
Coleus
Dandelion
Donkey's Tail
Fir (Christmas) Tree
Jade Plant
Kolanchoe
Spider Plant
Swedish Ivy
Wandering Jew

Mirrors and windows pose a special threat to flighted birds, who can crash into them.

used to keep things from sticking to the pan, are released at a temperature of 530°F (297°C) or hotter. This is hotter than the heat that most people cook with, so you may know people who have cooked with nonstick cookware with no apparent ill effects to their birds. But a pan that is forgotten and allowed to boil dry can easily reach much higher temperatures than are normally used in cooking.

Birds that are exposed to PTFE fumes often show no symptoms of it until they fall off the perch—dead. PTFE is also sometimes used to coat the inside of nonstick ovens, electric grills and skillets, the drip pans that surround the burners on stove tops, to line the inside of some hair driers, on irons, and more. Owners should be careful to remove their birds from the area when using products that contain PTFE.

In the Bathroom

Bathrooms hold several potential dangers for lovebirds. Toilet seats should be kept down so that the birds cannot accidentally fall into them and drown. All medications and cosmetics should be kept in their containers and in the medicine cabinet. Some lovebirds like to shower in the sink, but care must be taken that they never venture into a full sink or tub.

In the Living Room

Ceiling fans pose a hazard to flighted birds. Cords can be chewed resulting in electric shock. An open fireplace may offer an inadvertent escape route and should be completely blocked off with a fireplace screen if your bird is out. Also, never run the vacuum cleaner while the bird is out of its cage. Because vegetable matter forms a natural part of a lovebird's diet, they consider any plant they can reach as fair game for tasting. See the table on page 55 for a list of which plants are safe or poisonous to your bird.

In the Bedroom

Be careful about leaving jewelry and beads around—a chewing lovebird will not only make short work of your jewelry, but may get a bead or jewel stuck in its throat and choke to death. Also, scented candles should not be used.

Other Dangers

Other Pets

Dogs, cats, and ferrets all pose great potential danger to pet birds. Birds are natural prey

Having an unsupervised bird loose on the floor puts both the bird and your belongings at risk.

for ferrets and cats and even a gentle dog may snap if bitten by an assertive lovebird, with fatal results. Lovebirds are too fearless for their own good and will act aggressively toward animals many times their size.

Of all of these, cats pose the greatest potential danger. Not only will a cat aggressively stalk and attack a lovebird, but even an unsuccessful attack may be fatal due to the bacteria in a cat's saliva. Even birds that appear to have survived a cat encounter unscathed should be seen by the veterinarian ASAP if there is any possibility that the cat's teeth may have pierced the bird's skin.

Even the gentlest dog or laziest cat should not be trusted with a pet lovebird. The bird itself may provoke a hostile reaction by going after the other pet and biting it. All it takes is one unguarded moment for tragedy to occur.

Loose Birds

Lovebirds outside their cages require very close supervision. Not only is there a risk of the bird going on the floor and being stepped on, but they are small and quick and if you are not paying attention you may discover that your bird is missing and you'll be amazed at just how many places in which a small bird can hide. An unsupervised lovebird can also do a fair amount of property damage, chewing wood in any form, including furniture and woodwork, and shredding any papers it comes across without regard to their importance. If your lovebird is outside its cage, you need to stay on your toes and be very vigilant.

Holiday decorations can be dangerous to lovebirds, who like to explore new things by tasting them.

Gripping the Bird

To clip a lovebird's wings, pick the bird up wrapped in a towel, making sure that the towel is safely over its head so that it cannot bite you. Be careful to hold the bird firmly, but not tightly, as it needs to be able to expand its lungs in order to breathe; because the bird has no diaphragm to make the lungs push air in and out, it needs to be able to expand and contract the chest muscles to do the job instead. If you grip the bird very tightly so that the chest can't expand, you may inadvertently asphyxiate it and kill it.

Expose the Wing

Once you have the bird securely held, gently pull the towel away from one side, exposing the wing. Grabbing the lower edge of the wing, carefully pull it out to the side (not up). Take a careful look at the wing. You should see several layers of feathers arranged in rows, the bottom layer of which are the longest feathers. These are called the *primary feathers.* Arrange the bird so that you hold it

Fan the feathers out so you can see each layer clearly.

around the body and catch the wing with your fingers so that the wing remains outstretched while you reach for the scissors. You will need to cut along the flight feathers that grow on the outer edge of the wing. Use the layer of feathers directly over this longest layer for a guide to where you should cut. Cut straight across the first five to seven of the longest feathers just below where they are covered by the next layer. Then shift the bird so that you expose the opposite wing and repeat the process. It's a good idea to ask your veterinarian or the breeder to show you how to do this the first time, or to be on hand to guide you the first time you attempt to do this yourself.

Flight

The bird will try to fly when you release it from the towel. Use this flight to judge the success of your clip job. If the bird flutters to the ground, you have done a good clip. If he drops like a stone, you either cut too many feathers or cut them too short. And if he can still fly, try again, cutting the next few primary feathers and/or cutting closer to the

WINGS

layer of feathers just above the primaries.

Don't Take the Bird Outside

Just because a bird is clipped does not make it safe for you to take the bird outside. Sometimes the wind will blow in just the right way so that it catches the bird in an updraft and it will take off for the trees, or the flight feathers will be grown in just enough without your realizing it so that the bird is able to fly. Being outside also increases the danger of a predator being able to catch your bird and make a meal out of it.

Use the layer of feathers directly over the longest layer as a guide to where you should cut.

How Long a Clip Job Will Last

It is impossible to predict exactly how long a clip job will last. If your bird was just in the process of molting and replacing its feathers, it will be able to fly again fairly soon. If you catch it after a recent molt, then the job will last longer.

You can tell a clipped bird from an unclipped one by looking at it when its wings are folded; if you can see the longer, round-tipped primary feathers sticking out at the end, the bird is unclipped. If you don't see them, then the bird has been clipped. Looking for their appearance is a good way of knowing when it's time to repeat the bird's clip job.

HEALTH

The two best things you can do to help your lovebird live a long and happy life are to provide it with good nutrition and to seek regular veterinary care.

It used to be believed that lovebirds would live for only a few years in captivity; however, with improved veterinary care and healthier diets, the life span of lovebirds has increased and may continue to do so as scientists learn more about the best way to care for a captive lovebird. Today, lovebirds can live as long as 15 to 20 years, with reports of individuals living even longer.

Avian Veterinarians

In the United States, any veterinarian can advertise that he or she will treat birds, but only a few have been specially trained in how to treat avian patients. These avian veterinarians have studied in depth the specific health needs of birds, have passed a special test, and are certified by the American Board of Veterinary Practitioners. When looking for a veterinarian for your bird, try to find one that is board certified in avian medicine.

A blue masked lovebird.

Vaccinations

Compared to a dog or a cat, there are very few diseases for which there are preventive vaccines for birds. Your veterinarian can tell you whether or not these vaccines are appropriate for your bird. In general, if you know and trust your breeder, the bird has not been exposed to other populations of birds, and comes from healthy stock, then it is unlikely that vaccinations will be necessary.

Signs of a Sick Bird

We discussed how to tell a sick-looking bird from a healthy-looking one in the section on choosing your lovebird—but appearances can be deceiving. Birds hide any visible symptoms of illness for as long as they can. You need to be vigilant and constantly look for signs that your bird might be ill.

Changes in behavior: These are often triggered by physical ailments. If your bird suddenly becomes irritable and tries to bite you, there may be a physical reason for it, such as

Like people, lovebirds sometimes get itchy, but that doesn't automatically mean your bird has mites.

an injury hidden beneath the feathers. If your bird stops eating or suddenly seems to become less active, ceases to vocalize, sneezes, vomits, has a nasal discharge, is missing feathers, spends its time huddled on the cage floor, or seems to spend an inordinate amount of time scratching itself, you should immediately seek veterinary advice.

Changes in the color, texture, or consistency of droppings: These may or may not be a sign of illness. Sometimes a particular food will change the appearance of a bird's droppings; for example, feeding the bird beets will cause the droppings to take on a reddish brown hue, while feeding an excessive amount of fruits will cause the droppings to be runny or wetter than usual. If you notice that your bird's droppings have changed, think back to determine if the change might be caused by something that it ate. If you aren't sure, feed the bird nothing but its regular diet for the next 24 hours; if healthy, the droppings should return to normal.

Other visible signs of illness: A bird may be ill if it sits on the bottom of the cage with its feathers puffed and its eyes closed. This is a sign of an advanced illness. If the bird sits on the bottom of the cage and appears to be straining, then you may have a hen that is having difficulty passing an egg. Either one of these conditions may be life-threatening and require prompt medical attention.

Drop in weight: Perhaps the most useful sign that a bird is ill is a sudden drop in weight. Because lovebirds are so small, you

Get medical care quickly if your lovebird is huddled on the floor with its eyes closed. This is a sure sign of a sick bird.

are not going to notice any weight change without a scale that measures in grams. One of the best things you can do to ensure your lovebird's health is to weigh it on a regular basis using a scale that gives the weight in grams on an LCD readout. Postal scales and diet scales can be very useful for this. Slight variations in weight are normal, but a consistent decrease in weight is a definite warning sign. Twice-weekly weigh-ins before you feed your bird are an excellent way of monitoring the bird's health.

The Hospital Box

Any bird that shows signs of illness should immediately be separated from your other birds and sanitary precautions similar to those used when you put your new bird in quarantine should be observed.

The hospital box is a special cage set aside for sick birds. It differs from a regular cage because it is smaller (thus easier to transport) and has solid sides instead of bars to prevent drafts from reaching the bird. In my house, we use the same small plastic carrying case that we use when we travel with Doodle; it was originally sold as a box for a hermit crab or lizard, but it has clear sides and a plastic top, and works well for our purposes.

✔ Line the bottom of the box with a folded dish towel (don't use a terrycloth towel, which may snag the bird's toenails) and cover this with a piece of paper towel; the white paper towel makes it easier to observe the bird's

droppings as well as making the box easier to clean. Small dishes of food and water should be added so that your bird can eat and drink if it feels up to it.

═══ CHECKLIST ═══

What to Have on Hand in Case of an Emergency

Tweezers
Hospital box
Heating pad
Eyedropper or syringe
Styptic stick to stop bleeding (cornstarch or flour may also be used in an emergency)
Towel
A pair of thick gloves
Your avian veterinarian's phone number

✔ Set half of the hospital box on top of a heating pad, checking the temperature inside the box frequently at first, but not leaving the thermometer inside the box with the bird (the mercury inside the thermometer is poisonous). Having only half of the box on the heating pad gives the bird a cooler place to move to in case it begins to feel overheated.

✔ Adjust the settings on the heating pad so that the temperature inside the box is between 85 and 90°F (29–32°C). Providing a warm environment allows the bird to use the energy it would normally spend maintaining its body temperature to fight off the illness.

✔ After the situation has been resolved, dispose of the paper towel and launder the cloth that served as the base pad as well as the cover of the heating pad.

✔ Disinfect the box with a solution of 1 part bleach to 10 parts hot water, then put the box away until the next time it's needed.

Emergencies

Emergencies are medical situations that are beyond the pet owner's ability to handle. The information given in this section is intended merely to keep the bird as safe and as comfortable as possible until you can get it to an animal hospital. These measures are not to be used in place of professional veterinary care.

Broken Bones

Do not try to splint broken bones or wings yourself or wait until they've healed. Unless they are set properly, your bird may become seriously disabled. If a break does occur, place the bird in the hospital box; the folded toweling on the bottom will provide some cushioning and allow you to move the bird without handling it and causing it further pain.

Poisoning

Lovebirds are aggressive chewers with no sense of their own mortality. It takes only an unguarded moment for a lovebird to eat something that is hazardous to its health. If this should happen, seek veterinary help immediately. If no veterinarian is available, try to encourage your bird to drink water in order to dilute the poison in its system. The American Society for the Prevention of Cruelty to Animals offers an Animal Poison Control Center with a hot line that you can contact if you can't reach your veterinarian promptly. They do charge a fee for this service, so if you do have to call, have your credit card handy. This hot line is available 24 hours a day, 7 days a week, 365 days a year at (888) 426-4435.

Diseases

The following diseases cannot be diagnosed or treated except by a trained veterinary professional, but they are covered here to help lovebird owners understand exactly what they are dealing with if they are ever unfortunate enough to have their lovebirds diagnosed as having one of these diseases.

Gram-negative Bacteria

There is always a certain amount of bacteria living inside the body; some of the bacteria is good—for example, it may help to digest the food that we eat—but other kinds of bacteria are bad, and they take a toll on the body. A Gram stain is a test in which a sample of the bird's droppings is analyzed and the amounts

A green pied peach-faced lovebird.

of the different bacteria present are counted. The good types of bacteria that are helpful are called "Gram-positive," while the types of bacteria that may cause illnesses are called "Gram-negative." It's normal for both Gram-positive and Gram-negative bacteria to be present in a bird's digestive system; the problem arises when there is too much Gram-negative bacteria present. If this is the case, the veterinarian will prescribe an antibiotic to reduce the number of Gram-negative bacteria living inside the bird.

Polyoma

Polyoma is a virus that can affect a bird at any age, but one that is particularly devastating to chicks and young lovebirds. It is almost always fatal in these younger birds, but adults are sometimes able to overcome this disease. Symptoms may include a darkening of the skin covering the abdomen, diarrhea, weight loss, shivering, and, in young birds, a continual crying. There is no known cure, but a vaccine to prevent polyoma is available. If polyoma is diagnosed, you should immediately disinfect every-

A creamino peach-faced lovebird.

thing that your bird comes into contact with in an attempt to eradicate the virus and stop all breeding activities until the crisis is passed.

Pacheco's Disease

Pacheco's disease is a virus that is also known as the Psittacine Herpes Virus. It is usually fatal, and the birds that do manage to survive often become carriers for the virus and may spread it to other birds within the home. A bird diagnosed with Pacheco's disease should be separated from other birds in the house as soon as possible and its environment, including dishes, perches, cage, toys, and anything else that the bird may have come into contact with, should be disinfected with a mixture of one part bleach to ten parts water. A vaccine is available but may cause an adverse reaction, and is generally given only if it's believed that a bird has been exposed to the virus or to a bird that carries the virus.

Proventricular Dilation Disorder

Proventricular Dilation Disorder, or PDD, is a particularly heartbreaking disease whose cause is unknown, although there are indications that it may be caused by a virus. It has been called "the wasting disease" in macaws because it is a long, chronic condition in which the bird may either eat voraciously but lose weight anyway, or stop eating, vomit, and pass undigested food in its droppings, leading to a severe weight loss. Although birds can be treated with steroids, there is no known cure and this condition is invariably fatal.

Psittacosis

Psittacosis is a particularly frightening disease because it is one of the few that can be transmitted from birds to humans, as well as to other birds. Sometimes referred to as "Parrot Fever" or "Chlamydiosis," this disease is quite contagious in unsanitary conditions and localized outbreaks of psittacosis may occur. This disease can be transmitted nasally, by exposure to the droppings or by breathing in the dust of the dried droppings from an infected bird. The organism that causes this disease can remain present and active within the bird's droppings for months and may be spread when the dust from dried droppings becomes airborne and is inhaled. Symptoms include the usual vague signs of illness: fatigue, watery eyes, sneezing, nasal discharge, weight loss, diarrhea, lime green droppings, and/or loss of appetite. If a person seeks medical attention while experiencing any of these symptoms, an atypical form of pneumonia, or a high fever, it is worth mentioning to the doctor that he or she has a bird at home. Psittacosis is diagnosed through the examination of a droppings culture, blood testing, or a DNA probe, but a false negative may result if the sample of droppings is one that was made while the bird was not shedding the virus. Fortunately, this illness is quite curable in the early stages with antibiotics.

Aspergillosis

Aspergillosis is caused by a fungus that takes hold in the air sacs, making breathing difficult. This condition is much more prevalent in birds that live in close contact with other birds or are kept in damp or unsanitary conditions, and is common among birds from other counties that were bred in those same conditions. Aspergillosis may be associated with an underlying illness, immuno-compromised birds or with a lack

of certain nutrients, such as vitamin A. It is treatable in its early stages, but is difficult to treat if the condition has been allowed to progress.

Psittacine Beak and Feather Disease

Psittacine Beak and Feather Disease, or PBFD, is one of the most devastating viruses that a bird owner can encounter. The most obvious symptom is feathers that come in twisted, broken, bent, or otherwise deformed. This virus is easily spread and may be quickly fatal to young birds. Older birds may be able to live a relatively normal life, but will be rather shocking in appearance, looking disheveled or bare with beak deformities. Immunostimulants can help improve the bird's quality of life and may also prolong it. These birds should be kept in isolation from other birds for the remainder of their days, and their owners should take care to keep the bird's living conditions as sanitary as possible in order to prevent the sick bird from possibly being exposed to other illnesses which it may not be able to fight.

Attention should also be given to the room temperature, because birds with PBFD may lack sufficient feather covering to keep their bodies warm. If your bird is diagnosed with this devastating condition, you need to remember that the virus can be transmitted on your skin or clothing, so you will need to change and bathe completely after spending time with your bird if you are going to go to a situation where there will be healthy birds present, such as a pet store or the home of a friend who has birds.

opposite page: A Fischer's lovebird.

Metal Toxicity

Just as human children can be poisoned by eating lead paint, lovebirds can also suffer from metal toxicity by exposure to zinc or lead, resulting in neurological damage. This damage can manifest itself as seizures, impaired balance, or jerky movements. Because lovebirds enjoy tasting and chewing everything they come across, they are at great risk for accidentally ingesting toxic metals, most notably lead and zinc.

If your bird is diagnosed with a metal toxicity, it is imperative that you try to locate the source of the poisoning in order to prevent further exposure. One of the leading sources of lead and zinc poisoning in birds is older or antique cages that used lead or zinc in the soldering to hold the cage together. Other possible sources of heavy metal poisoning may include paint chips or items that were painted with a lead-based paint before the health risks were known, as well as some jewelry, linoleum, fishing weights, batteries, and some bells. If you are not sure what type of metal an item is made of, the safest thing is to remove that item from your bird's environment.

Diarrhea and Polyuria

Although these are not diseases but symptoms, they may be your first indication of a serious health problem; if the conditions persist, they may lead to dehydration and possibly even to seizures and death. Diarrhea in birds manifests itself as extremely runny, watery, and possibly off-colored droppings. Polyuria is an increase in the amount of urine and urates produced by the kidneys. Because the birds absorb most of the liquid that they ingest, the urine is normally passed as the white portion of the birds droppings. Although most people think abnormal droppings are automatically diarrhea, polyuria is often mistaken for diarrhea and is actually much more common. Droppings may also appear watery or runny as a result of the bird eating certain foods.

If you suspect an unusual food item may be the cause of a change in droppings, remove that food and replace the lining on the floor of the cage. If subsequent droppings do not return to normal within a few hours, or if the bird is exhibiting other signs of illness, such as sitting on the bottom of the cage or puffed feathers, get veterinary help promptly. In the event that veterinary help is not immediately available, you can try to give your bird something to soothe its digestive tract, such as boiled white rice or warm (not hot and not cold) chamomile tea (never give a bird tea or any other drink that contains caffeine), but these are not to be used in the place of professional medical attention.

Mites

Mites in birds are similar to lice in humans; they are small red insects that burrow beneath a bird's feathers and will bite the bird and suck its blood, causing the bird great discomfort and anemia. If you notice your bird scratching incessantly, squealing suddenly as if in pain, or biting at or pulling out its feathers, mites may be the cause.

It's very hard to see mites burrowing in the feathers. To check for mites, place a plain sheet of white paper on the cage floor early in the evening. Mites are most active at night, so check the white paper just before you go to bed. If you see small red dots on the paper,

these are mites that have fallen off the bird. Commercial sprays to get rid of mites work well. Follow the manufacturer's directions and clean the cage and the bird's belongings thoroughly before you spray the bird; running the belongings through hot water in the dishwasher is an easy way to accomplish this (but be careful if parts of your bird's cage are made of plastic—very hot water may melt them).

Many pet stores sell "mite repellent," small containers that you hang on the side of the bird's cage to prevent mites from infesting your bird, but these are a waste of money if you have a healthy, mite-free bird. Your bird will get mites only if it is exposed to another bird that is infested with them, so these mite repellents are not necessary.

Feather Plucking

Unlike some other parrots, lovebirds are not notorious for pulling out all of their feathers until they are left with bare patches on their bodies, but it is not unheard of either. Although there are many causes of plucking—mites, malnutrition, emotional stress, boredom, etc.—it is very important that the cause be identified and eliminated as soon as possible. If allowed to persist, pulling out its own feathers can become a habit rather than a symptom, and while the cause of the condition may be easily cured, it is much harder to eliminate a habit.

Feather plucking is observed when you see the bird pulling out its own feathers to the point where bald patches result. If you see your bird with a feather in its mouth but no bald spots, don't panic—lovebirds will regularly pull out individual feathers as part of their grooming process, making room for the new feathers that are coming through. If your lovebird is bald on its head, then it is either being plucked by another bird or has some other condition that is causing its feathers to fall out, because the bird cannot reach to pluck its own head.

If you have a lovebird that plucks, take it to the veterinarian to check for physical causes. If none are found, try moving the cage to a less trafficked area of the house to see if this reduces any stress the bird might be feeling. Check your bird's diet to make sure that it's digesting a wide variety of vitamins and minerals and not eating only seed mix. Try to provide a new assortment of toys to engage the bird's attention and help to keep it from being bored, and every time you catch the bird in the act of pulling a feather, tell it to stop and start to interact with it as a way of distracting it. In extreme cases, your veterinarian may want to put a collar around your bird's neck to prevent it from reaching its own feathers in order to give the new feathers a chance to come in, although this can be very traumatic for the bird.

Blood Feathers

As feathers grow in, there is a blood supply that flows into the shaft as the shaft breaks through the skin and begins to grow. These "blood feathers" can be recognized because the blood appears as a dark blue-purple color inside the shaft, close to the skin. Ordinarily these present no problem and the blood supply diminishes and ceases as the feather grows. However, if the blood feather is cut or broken, the feather will start to bleed. This can happen either during a wing trim or as the result of a feather being broken by a fall or because of a bite from another bird. Sometimes the

Removing old feathers as new ones grow in is normal; large patches of featherless skin is not.

broken blood feather will clot and cease to bleed on its own but if this is not the case, it is necessary for the owner to stop the bleeding by pulling out the broken feather.

To remove a bleeding blood feather, grasp the shaft firmly just above the skin line, either with pliers, tweezers, a hemostat, or with your fingers if your hands are clean. Pull the shaft up and out with a twisting motion. Removing the feather will cause some pain, similar to what you would feel if someone pulled out one of your hairs, so you may want to cover the bird's head with a towel and have someone else hold your lovebird while you do this. If there is any residual bleeding after you pull the blood feather, you can stop it with a styptic stick or by applying cornstarch to encourage the wound to clot.

BREEDING LOVEBIRDS

Breeding lovebirds is not something that should be entered into lightly. To raise handfed, well-socialized lovebirds can be expensive, time-consuming, and frustrating, and there is no guarantee of success. There are many things that can go wrong that may result in the death of the hen or chicks or both, but if you are careful, conscientious, and go into it for the right reasons, you may be in for one of the most fascinating, rewarding experiences of your life.

There are basically three ways that people start breeding lovebirds. The first occurs when a person proceeds after doing a great deal of research and giving the matter a lot of consideration. The second way is for a person to go into breeding on a whim, perhaps mistakenly thinking that breeding lovebirds is a way to make a quick buck. In the third way, it never occurs to the owner to breed lovebirds at all—it's entirely the bird's idea.

To Breed, or Not to Breed

There are many reasons why you might want to try breeding lovebirds and almost as many reasons not to. Reasons that you might want

A female lovebird may lay eggs whether or not she has access to a male or a nest box.

to start breeding lovebirds include an interest in trying to achieve different color mutations, an interest in showing lovebirds competitively, having friends who adore your bird and would like to own one of its offspring, wanting to experience the excitement of following the life cycle of a lovebird from egg to adult, or wanting to help perpetuate a rare species (although this is something best left to experienced aviculturalists).

Reasons that you might *not* want to breed lovebirds include a health risk to your bird (it is not unheard of for a hen to be unable to successfully deliver an egg and to die as a result), a large commitment of time (if you want to have handfed babies, you need to be available to handfeed them around the clock, if necessary, and definitely every few hours during the daylight hours, including the

A masked lovebird building its nest. The upper compartment serves as entrance hall with nest opening. The lower compartment is the true nest where the young are hatched and raised.

workday), a fairly large expense—you will need to invest in nest boxes and cages for the new birds, as well as baby formula, a thermometer and syringes for handfeeding, with the possibility of veterinary bills as well—and the distinct possibility that you will not be able to find a new home for your babies, resulting in more birds than you really wanted to own.

Also, if you have a cherished pet lovebird that is both interactive and affectionate with you, be aware that adding a mate will change your social dynamic and that if you set her up to breed, she will become very protective of her nest and eggs and aggressive toward you for as long as she is raising the chicks.

Profits

Visions of a healthy profit are not realistic. While some of the bigger species of parrots may fetch thousands of dollars for a single, handfed bird, lovebirds are fairly plentiful in captivity and most breed regularly enough so that they do not command the high prices of some other types of birds.

Breeding Basics

Before you begin, you need to know for sure that you have a male and a female. Although there are people who claim that they can tell a male from a female simply by examining the bird's physical characteristics, this is not a reliable method of determining a bird's gender in most species. While it is true that the female lovebird has a slightly wider pelvic area than the male to allow the eggs to pass through her body, this is a difference of mere millimeters and is too small to be accurately assessed by simply looking at or feeling it.

Unless you have a sexually dimorphic species of lovebird (one where the males and females look distinguishably different), there are three ways to be sure of a lovebird's gender.

1. If your bird lays an egg, that is a sure sign that you have a hen rather than a cock.

2. Another option is surgical sexing—having the veterinarian anesthetize the bird so that he or she can insert a laparoscope and visually examine the bird's sex organs, but this method is invasive and not without risk to the bird.

3. The most common way of determining gender is to have the bird DNA sexed. This is a procedure in which a small sample of blood or tissue, usually taken from a blood sample or a freshly plucked chest feather, is analyzed in a lab to determine if the bird has the DNA of a male or a female. These tests can be performed using a home test kit where the owner gathers the sample and sends it to the lab for the results, or by visiting the veterinarian's office and asking him or her to take and send in the sample for you. The results are usually back within a few weeks.

Important: It's very important that you do not try to cross the different lovebird species

The lovebird will line the nest with whatever material is available to cushion the eggs.

in your attempts to breed lovebirds. The babies, called "hybrids," tend to not be as healthy as the purebred specimens, and lovebirds of different species are less likely to be compatible than two individuals of the same species.

If you are introducing a new lovebird to your own bird with an eye to breeding them, it's important to observe quarantine before you introduce the two. It's very important that the birds be in optimum health before they begin their reproductive efforts. Provide as varied and healthy a diet as possible, including plenty of fresh vegetables. Make sure the hen has access to a mineral block or cuttlebone in order to allow her sufficient calcium to produce her eggs. When you are ready to introduce them, follow the procedures outlined in the section, Adding a Second Bird (page 37).

The Nest Box

Lovebirds in the wild do not build nests the way we usually think of a bird building a nest. Instead, they find a convenient hollow in a tree or under the tiles of a roof or in an abandoned swift's nest and they proceed to take over that space as their own, carrying back a variety of different materials to shred and line the interior space.

To encourage your lovebirds to breed, you need to offer them a suitable substitute to

nest in. A small wooden box with a 2- to 3-inch (5.1–7.6 cm) hole high up on one of the sides, and a hinged top, should be provided. Nest boxes sold for budgies and cockatiels both work well for lovebirds. If you decide to

After a period of courtship, actual mating begins when the male bird mounts the female.

You'll need to provide at least one nest box per lovebird pair.

make one yourself, pine is a good wood to use. The dimensions of the box are not important as long as there is sufficient room for the lovebird to sit and turn around within its confines, and the cage should be big enough to accommodate both parents and the nest box. The nest box can either be mounted outside the cage with its entrance lined up with an opening in the cage bars, or inside it.

Being an avid chewer, your lovebird will probably chew on the opening or on the floor and sides of the box in an effort to get it to their liking. I usually place a layer of pine shavings on the bottom of the nest box to help cushion the eggs and keep them from rolling around, and to make the nest box easier to clean as the babies hatch and begin voiding inside the box (do not use cedar or corncob bedding for this). Because a chick's legs may become deformed ("splay legged") from sitting directly on the hard wooden floor of the nest box, make sure that this layer of shavings is at least 2–3 inches (5.1–7.6 cm) thick in order to provide a suitable cushion for the chicks. The lovebird may chew on these woodchips or even discard them from the nest if they are not to her liking. I provide crumpled-up paper towels on the cage floor for the birds to shred and carry back to their nests as a lining.

The lovebirds will be very diligent about working their nest boxes and will become very protective of them. If you have more than one pair of lovebirds, you will either need to provide nest boxes for all of the pairs, or make sure that the pair you intend to breed have a cage to themselves.

Change in Attitude

You will probably notice a marked change in your lovebird's attitude toward you once it has a nest box. It will become very protective and will aggressively object if you try to reach into the cage. Do not worry about cleaning out the inside; the hen will leave the box to defecate, and sanitation will not be a problem until after the babies start to hatch.

Location of Nest Box

Many people like to mount the nest box high on the sides of the cage to simulate placement in a tree, but this isn't necessary. If the cage is wide but short, the lovebirds will use a nest box placed on the floor of the cage as readily as one placed high up, although you may find that droppings from the male accumulate on the roof of the nest box if it is placed down low.

Birds and Sex

If you are new to breeding birds, you may be wondering just how birds—*ahem*—do it. The answer is, often and with a great sense of balance. In the days prior to mating, you may notice that the birds are even closer than usual, preparing the nest box together and feeding each other regularly. It is the female that seems to determine when it is time to mate. If the male makes an advance before she is ready, she will rebuff him in no uncertain terms. When she is ready, she will lower her head and raise her tail until she is in what looks like a crouch. The male will climb onto her back, and carefully maneuver so that his vent area rubs against hers. The job done, he dismounts and both birds will set about putting themselves back in order, preening and observing each other with what looks like great satisfaction.

Not all copulation will result in fertile eggs, nor do the birds have to copulate for eggs to be laid. Many a lovebird owner has discovered their bird's true gender by the sudden appearance of an egg in the bottom of the cage. Eggs laid by females that have not had access to a male are infertile and have no chance of hatching, but the hen may be just as protective and nurturing as any other expectant mother.

If this is the case with your bird, the best thing to do is to leave her to sit on the eggs. They will not hatch, but if you remove them, she will likely lay more to replace them, taking a toll on her physically. After about a month she will seem to realize that they are not going to hatch and will abandon them, at which point you can remove them from the cage. Although she will be very aggressive toward you for as long as she is sitting on them, she should become as manageable as she was before laying after the cycle has run its course as long as there is no male bird present.

Egg Bound

If you notice a female lovebird that seems to be sitting on the bottom of the cage crouched and straining, she may be trying to pass an egg that, for whatever reason, is "stuck" inside her. To check, carefully pick the hen up (I recommend wearing gloves to do this, as she is not going to appreciate your efforts) and look at her vent area. If it is open and swollen or you can see the white of a shell, then you have a serious situation on your hands. This condition, called "egg bound," can have fatal results. Do not try to break the egg inside her to make it easier to pass because doing so could puncture her insides, which would also be fatal. *Get veterinary help right away.* If there is going to be a delay in getting to the veterinarian, place the bird in a hospital box with a heating pad; the warmth will sometimes help the muscles relax to the point where the egg will be able to pass. You can also try to rub a little warm baby oil or vegetable oil around the outer edge of the vent to help the egg pass.

This condition is extremely serious. There are several possible causes, but the most preventable one is malnutrition. Make sure that your pet has a good, varied diet that includes vegetables and has access to a cuttlebone or mineral block at all times.

Laying Eggs

The eggs are laid about a week to ten days after copulation. Hens usually lay one egg every other day or so until there are four to seven eggs in the nest. Very often the hen will not sit on them until she has two or three in the nest. This is a good thing. By delaying incubation, she delays the process of chick development, so that if she waits until she has three eggs before sitting, all three will hatch at approximately the same time. Baby lovebirds grow astoundingly fast, and there can be a terrific size difference between chicks that hatch just two days apart. If the chicks hatch at about the same time, they are better equipped to compete with their siblings to be fed. It is not uncommon for the youngest and smallest chicks to be unable to compete with their much bigger siblings for food, so they starve to death.

In most cases, the hen sits on the eggs and the male feeds her (the blackmasked lovebird may be an exception to this). If the hen is laying without a mate, she will usually hurriedly leave the eggs alone while she eats and defecates, quickly returning to brood.

Not all mating or egg laying will result in chicks. There are many different causes for nonhatching eggs, including infertility, parents abandoning the nest, illness, accidents, and malnutrition. If a first attempt at breeding lovebirds is unsuccessful and it is still something that you really want to try, remove the nest box and unhatched eggs so that your hen will have a chance to rest and regain her strength, and try again after three months have passed.

Chronic Egg Laying

Lovebirds are more likely to lay eggs in the spring or summer months, when the weather is warm and the daylight hours are longer, but artificial heat and lighting throw some birds'

Although this blue peach-faced/blue masked lovebird is an attractive hybrid, crossbreeding is discouraged.

internal clocks off, fooling them into thinking it's time to reproduce.

Chronic egg laying can occur with either a single hen or a pair. If your bird lays eggs more than every four to six months, the strain of producing these eggs is going to take a toll on her body, possibly even shortening her life. There are several things you can do to discourage chronic egg laying:

✔ First, if your bird lays eggs, do not remove them from the cage; let her sit and incubate them. Sitting on one batch of eggs will keep her from producing another to replace them.

✔ Try to limit the number of hours your bird is exposed to light; long days make the bird more likely to breed, so turn off the lights at 8:00 P.M., and if you cover your bird's cage, don't uncover it until 8 A.M. This may fool your bird into thinking that it's winter and not a suitable time to breed.

✔ Relocating the cage (or even changing the bird from one cage to another) every other week or so may also leave the bird just unsettled enough so that it doesn't lay eggs.

In an extreme case, you may need to consult a veterinarian about hormone shots or even having the bird's ovaries surgically removed, although these are extreme measures and should be considered only as a last resort. It is also particularly important to provide good nutrition and a source of calcium if you have a chronic egg layer, because she will need to replace the reserves that she uses in forming her eggs.

One aberration that sometimes happens in captivity is that a pair of lovebirds form a close, affectionate bond and even work the nest together, but when the owner checks the nest, he or she discovers not one but two birds sitting and realizes that there are an extraordinary number of eggs present, far more than the four to seven that might be expected. If this is the case, the chances are that your "pair" is not a mated cock and hen, but a pair of cohabitating hens, both of whom are sharing the nest box and laying eggs at the same time. Because there's no male present, none of these eggs will be fertile or hatch. As long as the hens do not squabble over the nest box space, you should leave them alone until they get tired of sitting and then remove the nest box from the cage, since they really don't need it.

Eggs of a peach-faced lovebird.

Lovebird chicks grow very quickly.

Lovebird chicks, such as these baby peach-faced, begin to show curiosity and individual personalities even before they're fully feathered.

Candling

Not all eggs laid by a lovebird will hatch. In many cases, and for many reasons, the hen may lay infertile eggs. You can try to determine if an egg is fertile or not by trying to shine a light through it. A "mag light" flashlight, where you can narrow the beam, works well for this. As the chick develops, you will first see red blood vessels, and then a dark portion of the egg that grows proportionally larger as the chick matures, finally filling up all of the shell except for the small air sack at the top.

Chicks

Lovebird eggs take approximately 21 to 26 days to hatch. While the eggs are incubating, the mother bird will usually take very good care of them, turning them frequently to allow the chick inside to develop normally. It's important that the eggs have some humidity, so if your area is very dry you should try to mist the mother bird while she is out of the nest box (misting directly inside the nest box may encourage mold growth among the bedding material).

As the hatch date nears, you may be able to hear peeping or tapping coming from inside the shell if you hold it up to your ear. The actual hatching may take anywhere from several hours to two days, because the chick needs to rest frequently. Do not attempt to assist the chick in breaking out of the shell unless you are quite sure that the chick is in distress—the chick needs to entirely absorb the yolk sack that is inside the egg before it hatches and it may become detached if you attempt to pull the shell away.

Newly hatched lovebird chicks are astonishingly ugly. They are born without feathers, but with faint wisps of white-yellow down on their bodies. Their eyes are closed and appear as dark blue globes beneath their eyelids, seeming to take up an astounding portion of their heads. They lift their heads to be fed, but otherwise tend to flop over, leaning against their siblings or the unhatched eggs for warmth.

The two front toes must be pointed forward to enable you to slip on the band.

Banding

There are two kinds of bands that can go on the bird's legs—open and closed. Open bands can be put on or removed at any time. Closed bands are put on when the bird is still a chick. They are put on over the bird's foot and as the bird grows, the band can be removed only by cutting it off (a job best left to a veterinarian).

Some people feel that banding should not be done because there is a chance that the bird will catch the band on something and injure its leg. Others feel that it's worth the risk because the identifying information on the back may some day help the owner recover a lost or stolen bird. Leg bands can be ordered through one of several companies that advertise in bird magazines and online. They can also be offered through some bird organizations. The information that goes on a leg band is decided by the owner or the organization that issues them. It may include identification numbers, the initials of the owner or organization, year of hatching, and/or the state in which the bird was hatched. It can also include the breeder's e-mail address or phone number.

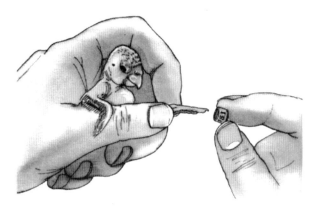

Handfeeding is a fairly simple operation in which much can go wrong. If at all possible, have someone who is experienced demonstrate exactly how to handfeed a new chick. This may not always be possible, but it is the easiest way.

Pulling the Chicks

The younger a chick is when it's pulled for handfeeding, the more likely it is not to survive. Most people who breed lovebirds wait until they are about two weeks old before "pulling" them from the nest to handfeed. This gives the birds a chance to grow larger, which makes them easier to feed. It is also safer for the chick to be fed by the parents initially, because the regurgitated

foods that the parents feed them will automatically be the right texture, consistency, and temperature for them. Lovebirds that were parent-hatched and fed naturally for the first days of their lives are also more likely to make successful parents themselves when they get older.

Age

If you have to handfeed, try to wait until the chicks are two weeks old before beginning. If you have to intervene with a younger bird for whatever reason, do so knowing that the odds are against you.

Technique

Begin with a commercial handfeeding formula and a 10 cc syringe (you may want

to buy these once you know you have fertile eggs, just in case). Follow the package directions to prepare it, making sure that it is between 103° and 105°F (39.4–40.5°C). If the mixture is too hot, you will burn the baby's crop; if it is too cold, the chick will not want to eat it. The younger the chick, the more watery the formula should be. Very young lovebirds hold very little formula, so begin with just a couple of cc's in the syringe.

✔ Arrange the baby so that it sits facing you.

✔ Take the syringeful of formula in your right hand and put it into the chick's mouth, going from right to left so that the end of the syringe is pointing to your left. This is important because if the formula goes down the wrong way, it will go into the chick's lungs instead of its crop, killing it.

✔ Slowly push the plunger of the syringe. Chicks normally pump their heads and chirp when their parents feed them, so expect the same behavior here. As the chick eats, you will see the crop, a pouchlike area under the throat, begin to fill and bulge.

✔ If the chick begins to refuse the formula, stop the

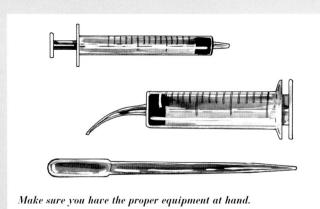

Make sure you have the proper equipment at hand.

CHICKS

feeding session. Baby chicks don't hold much, and overfeeding them could cause them to aspirate the formula into their lungs and die.

✔ Wipe off any excess formula that may have missed the mouth and return the chick to its warm resting place (an arrangement similar to the sick box works well for chicks that have been pulled).

Young chicks need to be fed every few hours around the clock. You will begin to recognize the peeping sound that they make when they are hungry.

Solid Food

As the chicks get older, they eat more formula less often. When they start to nibble on things, it's time to begin to offer them "solid" food. Begin with warm cooked and mashed vegetables, offering them with your fingertips. As they get older, gradually introduce seed mix

Be careful to point the syringe from right to left. If you point it the wrong way, the formula can be injected into the chick's lungs.

or pellets, leaving them in a dish for the chicks to pick at. As they eat more "big bird" food, they will take less and less formula, and you can ease back on the handfeedings, offering to feed them less and less often until it is gradually eliminated.

UNDERSTANDING YOUR LOVEBIRD'S BODY LANGUAGE

Even though a lovebird may not speak, it still manages to convey a wide variety of needs and emotions through its actions and body language, if the owner is perceptive enough to interpret them.

Beak Grinding

Many times, in the evening, owners will hear a faint abrasive noise and look over to see their bird standing on the perch, slightly puffy, grinding its beak. This is normal. Like many other parrots, lovebirds grind their beaks when they are sleepy as part of their settling down for the night. This action does not signify that there is anything wrong or that the beak needs to be trimmed; it's just a sign of a sleepy, contented bird.

Even birds that don't talk are able to communicate through behavior and body language.

Blinking

As mentioned previously, a predator that is stalking a bird in the wild will stare at it unrelentingly. Blinking is a way of breaking the stare, and lovebirds will blink as a way of reassuring each other that they are safe and that there is no danger present. They may also use it as a sign of affection. Blinking at a new bird is a good, nonverbal way of making it feel safe.

Wing Flapping

Birds that stand on their perch and flap their wings rapidly are merely exercising. This is a sign of a healthy, active bird and is more common among birds that are clipped or that

Lovebirds at a Glance

(1 millimeter = .0394 inches; 1 gram = 0.0353 ounces)

Species	Length (mm)	Wing (mm)	Tail (mm)	Beak (mm)	Tarsus (mm)
Agapornis cana	130–140	91–101	41–50	11–12	12–13
A. c. ablectanea	135–143	90–101	44–54	11–12	12–14
A. personata fischeri	140–150	90–95	40	15–18	14–15
A. p. lilianae	130–140	70	40	14–15	14
A. p. nigrigenis	130–140	92–93	45	14–15	13–14
A. p. personata	150–157	90–98	39–45	13–14	12–14
A. pullaria pullaria	130–150	83–98	35–41	13–15	9–12
A. p. ugandae	130–148	87–95	34–41	13–15	12–13
A. roseicollis roseicollis	160–180	100–110	45–55	17–18	13–14
A. r. catumbella	150–170	99–105	43–47	17–18	14–16
A. swinderniana swinderniana	130–140	88–94	32–36	12–14	11–13
A. s. emini	130–150	89–97	31–35	12–14	12–14
A. taranta taranta	150–165	95–106	41–52	17–18	14–15

spend the majority of their time in a cage and are not able to exercise by making long flights.

Head Bobbing

A very young bird that bobs its head up and down may be asking to be fed. A mother lovebird (or, less often, the father) feeds its young by placing her beak over the baby's beak and bringing up food from her crop by making a vigorous bobbing motion. In older birds, feeding each other is a sign of affection between a bonded pair and the food is brought up in much the same way. If you have a single love-bird and observe this behavior, it may well be that the bird is expressing its affection for *you*. Some birds may even manage to bring up some regurgitated food for you. Try to react positively. Coming from your bird, this is the ultimate compliment.

Head Bowing

A lovebird that lowers its head almost to the point where the forehead touches the floor is inviting you to help make it feel more comfortable by preening the feathers on the back of its head and neck. When new feathers first

| Weight (grams) | | Weight/Eggs | Dimensions/Eggs | Incubation |
Male	Hen	(grams)	(mm)	(Days)
24–29	24–29	3.2	19–20 × 16–17	21–22
?	?	?	?	?
40–49	45–53	3.3	20–24.5 × 16.5–18	21–24
36–38	34–43	3.25	21.5–22 × 16–17	21–25
36–38	45–52	3.25	21.5–22 × 16.5–18	16–21
43–52	±56	3.5–4.0	21.5–25.5 × 17–18	21–23
36–43	36–43	4.0	20–22 × 16–17	21–22
36–44	35–44	4.1	19.7–22.3 × 15.8–17.3	21–22
±45	±50	3.5	21–25 × 17–19	21–22
±44	±50	3.5	29.8–25.2 × 17.2–19.1	21–22
±35	±35	?	?	?
±36	±36	?	?	?
±65	±55	?	?	24–26

poke through the skin, they can be quite itchy, and as the feathers emerge further, they need to have the waxy covering opened to allow the barbules to stand out from the quill. Scratching your bird's head and neck is one of the best ways to build a positive owner-pet bond.

Paper Shredding and Tucking

This activity is more common in females than in males, although some males do engage in it. The lovebird will take any kinds of papers—loose sheets, envelopes, newspapers, the lining on the bottom of the cage, even paperback novels—and will carefully chew off a long narrow strip. The bird then takes these strips and carefully tucks them between her feathers and when she has accumulated quite a few of them, she flies off to her cage with them.

This rather destructive habit means that your bird is feeling the impulse to set up a nest and breed, and the strips of paper are intended to be used as part of a lining for a nest. Although lovebirds usually nest in hollows of trees, many lovebirds will set up their "nest" inside a food dish or even on the bare bottom of the cage. If a strip or two is lost in flight, the bird will

Blue and black-faced lovebirds.

Puffed feathers may indicate that a lovebird is trying to adjust its body temperature. A momentary puffing is simply the bird stretching or putting its feathers in order.

Lovebirds can be a friendly and interactive pet.

merely fly back to the source to replace them later. You may also notice that your bird becomes more irritable and inclined to nip at about the same time she begins to shred paper. This is due to the increased level of hormones, which may result in moodiness.

Puffed Feathers

A bird with puffed-up feathers may be uncomfortable with the temperature of the room or this may be a sign that your bird is seriously ill. If you see a lovebird with puffed feathers, particularly if it's on the bottom of the cage with closed or glazed-looking eyes, seek veterinary help immediately. Birds in the wild live by the code of "survival of the fittest"—a predator will single out a young or sickly looking bird as possibly being easier to catch. Consequently, a bird will hide any signs of illness for as long as it is able to. By the time you notice the bird on the cage floor with puffed feathers, it is already far gone in its illness, and it may already be too late to help it.

This habit of hiding illnesses for as long as possible is one of the things that make people think of birds as fragile, because they think the bird looks healthy until the very end of the illness when it seems to die suddenly. In fact, illnesses may be ongoing for quite a while before the bird exhibits any noticeable symptoms.

Tail Rubbing

Some birds will vigorously rub their lower abdomen against a perch or a toy or some other hard surface, swishing their tails back and forth rapidly as they do so. If you observe this behavior, your bird is most likely a male. This behavior is the bird's way of masturbating, or relieving some of the built-up sexual urges that he's feeling. Although it may be a little embarrassing to explain to Grandma that this is what he's doing, it's actually a healthy activity for him and should be allowed to continue.

Head on Back

It looks decidedly uncomfortable. A lovebird will be sitting on its perch with its head twisted all the way around so that it's chin rests on its back. Lovebirds often sleep this way, with their heads supported by their backs.

Body Crouched, Wings Spread

If water is running somewhere in the house, or the vacuum cleaner is going, you may notice your lovebird holding a strange position. The head will be down, the wing raised, and the feathers may be slightly puffed out. This is the bird's way of saying that it wants to get wet, so you should oblige by offering a dish of water to splash in or spraying it with a plant mister. Birds that are reluctant to bathe can often be encouraged by hearing the sound of running water or a vacuum cleaner.

Where to Find Each Species of Lovebird in the Wild

Peach-faced lovebirds

Black-cheeked lovebirds

Madagascar lovebirds

Masked lovebirds

Nyasa lovebirds

Red-faced lovebirds

Fischer's lovebirds

Abyssinian lovebirds

*Swindern's lovebirds
(Black-collared lovebirds)*

INFORMATION

Books

Appleyard, Vera. *The Lovebird Handbook.* Hauppauge, NY: Barron's Educational Series, Inc., 2001.

Athan, Mattie Sue. *Guide to a Well-Behaved Parrot.* Hauppauge, NY: Barron's Educational Series, Inc., 1999.

D'Angieri, Alessandro. *The Colored Atlas of Lovebirds.* Neptune, NJ: TFH Publications, 1997.

McWatters, Alicia. *A Guide to a Naturally Healthy Bird: Nutrition, Feeding, and Natural Healthy Methods for Parrots.* Sheffield, MA: New Century Publishing, 1997.

Periodicals

Bird Talk Magazine
3 Burroughs
Irvine, CA 92618
http://www.animalnetwork.com/birdtalk/

Companion Parrot Quarterly
PBIC Inc
PO Box 2428
Alameda, CA 94501-0254
http://www.companionparrot.com

Bird Times
Pet Publishing, Inc.
7-L Dundas Circle
Greensboro, NC 27407
http://www.petpublishing.com/birdtimes/

Organizations

The African Lovebird Society
Attn: Club Affiliation
P.O. Box 142
San Marcos, CA 92079
http://www.africanlovebirdsociety.com

Association of Avian Veterinarians
P.O. Box 811720
Boca Raton, FL 33481-1720
(561) 393-8901
http://www.aav.org

Yellow Fischer's lovebird.

Peach-faced lovebird.

I N D E X

About the Author

Mary Gorman is a freelance writer specializing in pet bird related topics. She has been published or quoted in *Ranger Rick, Bird Talk, Companion Parrot Quarterly, Bird Times, Original Flying Machine,* and *Birds USA.* Although she owned a couple of pairs of lovebirds in the 1980's, these days she specializes in pionus parrots and owns a single pet lovebird hen. Mary holds a Master's degree in English literature from the University of Massachusetts at Amherst.

Photo Credits

B. Everett Webb: pages 3, 4, 5, 8, 9, 11, 12, 13 (left), 14, 16, 17, 19, 20, 25, 27, 28, 29, 32, 33, 35, 36, 38, 40, 41, 43, 44 (bottom left & right), 48, 49 (top), 53, 56, 57 (bottom), 60, 61, 62, 65, 66, 68, 71, 72, 73, 75, 76, 79, 80, 84, 85, 88, 89, 92; Robert Pearcy: 13 (right), 24, 44 (top left), 52, 57 (top), 93; Rainer Erhart: 21, 44 (top right), 51; Reinhardt: 49 (bottom).

Cover Photos

Front cover by Robert and Eunice Pearsay.
Back and inside front and back covers by B. Everett Webb.

Important Note
This book deals with the care and maintenance of lovebirds. People who are allergic to feathers or feather dust should not keep birds. If you are not sure whether you might have such a bird allergy, consult a doctor before buying birds.

When birds are handled, they sometimes bite and scratch. Have such wounds immediately treated by a physician.

Although psittacosis is not common among lovebirds, it can produce symptoms in both humans and birds and be very serious. If you have any reason to suspect psittacosis, and have flu or cold symptoms, see a doctor immediately.

Dedication

For my grandmother, Elizabeth Lynch DiSciullo, and her brother William Lynch for their love, support and wisdom. Who knew what your backyard birdfeeders would lead to?

Acknowledgment

Special thanks to Dr. Marjorie McMillan, DVM, of Windhover Veterinary Center, avian vet extraordinaire, for watching over the flock and for reviewing the health chapter of this book prior to publication.

All inquiries should be addressed to:
Barron's Educational Series, Inc.
250 Wireless Boulevard
Hauppauge, NY 11788
www.barronseduc.com

ISBN-13: 978-0-7641-3062-5
ISBN-10: 0-7641-3062-5

Library of Congress Catalog Card No. 2004052976

Library of Congress Cataloging-in-Publication Data
Gorman, Mary.
   Lovebirds: a complete pet owners manual /
by Mary Gorman.
      p. cm.
   ISBN 0-7641-3062-5
   1. Lovebirds. I. Title.

SF473.L6G67 2005
636.6'864—dc22   2004052976

Printed in China
9 8 7 6 5